C000026322

MAN STUFF

A BOOK FOR BLOKES

RAY HAMILTON

summersdale

MAN STUFF

Copyright © Summersdale Publishers Ltd, 2019

All rights reserved.

No part of this book may be reproduced by any means, nor transmitted, nor translated into a machine language, without the written permission of the publishers.

Ray Hamilton has asserted his moral right to be identified as the author of this work in accordance with sections 77 and 78 of the Copyright, Designs and Patents Act 1988.

Condition of Sale
This book is sold subject to the condition that it shall not, by way of trade or otherwise, be lent, resold, hired out or otherwise circulated in any form of binding or cover other than that in which it is published and without a similar condition including this condition being imposed on the subsequent purchaser.

An Hachette UK Company
www.hachette.co.uk

Summersdale Publishers Ltd
Part of Octopus Publishing Group Limited
Carmelite House
50 Victoria Embankment
LONDON
EC4Y 0DZ
UK

www.summersdale.com

Printed and bound in the Czech Republic

ISBN: 978-1-78685-794-1

Substantial discounts on bulk quantities of Summersdale books are available to corporations, professional associations and other organisations. For details contact general enquiries by telephone: +44 (0) 1243 771107 or email: enquiries@summersdale.com

CONTENTS

INTRODUCTION

I've been trying to become a man all my life, with varying degrees of success. I have picked up some man stuff along the way, though, and I'm happy to share that stuff with you in this book. From ideas on how to travel in ever-more-adventurous ways to how to mix the perfect beer cocktail, from tips on how to stay happy and healthy to the best method to skin a racoon for your supper (I might have made that last bit up), there's something in here for men of all ages, interests and skill levels. If you need to brush up on your general knowledge, or learn how to dress for different occasions, or be a better cook, or fix stuff, this is the book for you. Honest.

We will also draw inspiration from great men in history and the modern age, from da Vinci to Darwin, Brunel to Banksy. On a personal level, I have been lucky enough to have as an added inspiration one of the best resources known to man: a big brother. Why is it that big brothers are always more practical than younger ones? Is it because they already had to fix stuff while their younger brothers were still kicking a ball around and there was nothing left to fix by the time we turned up wielding our first hammer? In any event, if you don't already have a big brother, I recommend that you get one.

It is particularly appropriate that I should have largely written *Man Stuff* during 2018 of all years, because it is a year in which I spent a fair amount of time in the wonderfully named Manly in New South Wales, Australia. I was there to play one of the manliest roles known to man, that of Father of the Bride, but I also picked up some other manly things to do in Manly while I was there. More of which later.

Ray Hamilton, February 2019

4

STUFF THAT MEN SHOULD KNOW

There's so much we have to know as men that it's hard to know where to start. Traditionally, we're supposed to know a lot of practical stuff, like how to build or fix things. I get that, and we'll come back to that practical stuff in the Man Skills and other chapters. But we also have to know about 'intellectual' stuff, because how else can we be expected to hold sensible conversations at dinner parties, or contribute meaningfully to quiz nights, or converse on an equal footing with our fellow men on male outings or at sporting events?

Perhaps we should start with which books to read, because there's a lot of manly knowledge to be had from books, as long as you choose the right ones.

BUILD UP YOUR MAN LIBRARY

Here are some suggestions to get your man library up and running:

The Compleat Angler (1653) by Izaak Walton: although first published almost 400 years ago, this remarkable book remains useful as a celebration of fishing, and is stuffed full of tips on how to catch and cook fish. It remains the most reprinted book in the English language after the Bible.

The Great Gatsby (1925) by F. Scott Fitzgerald: infused with the decadence of 1920s east-coast America, this is the story of a man who reinvents himself to win back the love of his life. If you ever had a first love, this will bring it all flooding back.

Guinness World Records (since 1955): a must-read because we all love world records, especially the one about *Guinness World Records* being the book most frequently stolen from public libraries.

Catch-22 (1961) by Joseph Heller: the cleverly structured and often comic novel tells the story of a US Air Force captain's experiences in World War Two and introduced 'catch-22' into the English language as a byword for an inescapable dilemma, like when you can't gain experience in your ideal job because you don't have the experience needed to get that ideal job in the first place.

The Man in the High Castle (1962) by Philip K. Dick: based on an alternative ending to World War Two, this book tells the story of daily life in the USA under the victorious but divisive powers of Imperial Japan and Nazi Germany. Since 2015 it has been the subject of a popular American TV series.

Zen and the Art of Motorcycle Maintenance (1974) by Robert Pirsig: ostensibly the fictitious story of a father and son on a motorcycle journey in 1970s America, but its views on quality of life, personal relationships and the human mind soon elevated it to classic status.

Watchmen (1986) by Alan Moore, Dave Gibbons and John Higgins: the world of alternative superheroes and moral struggles depicted in this limited series turned comic books into a legitimate literary genre.

The ***SAS Survival Handbook*** (since 1986) by John 'Lofty' Wiseman or the ***US Army Survival Manual*** (since 1956) issued by the US Department of Defense: they both have all the tips you could ever need to prepare relevant equipment, defend yourself in any situation, find food on land or sea and navigate through every kind of environment known to man.

Commando Dad (2012) by Neil Sinclair: this survival advice for new recruits to fatherhood has been written by ex-Commando and father-of-three Neil Sinclair, who is ideally placed to advise on everything from setting up base camp to surviving the first difficult years of fatherhood.

ARTY GUYS

While we're on a bit of a culture kick, let's have a look at some famous men in the world of art:

Michelangelo: the artist and sculptor responsible for the ceiling of the Sistine Chapel and the painting of *The Last Judgement* had already produced the awe-inspiring *Pietà* and *David* sculptures by the time he was 30.

Leonardo da Vinci: the Renaissance master who gave us the world's most famous painting, the *Mona Lisa*. The portrait of the Italian noblewoman and her enigmatic smile is worth the entrance money to the Louvre alone. (Da Vinci was much more than a painter, of course, so we'll be returning to this polymath of polymaths in the Man Skills chapter.)

Peter Paul Rubens: the artist who has had us admiring the fuller, more-rounded version of the female form for 400 years, at least until Twiggy came along and spoiled it for him in the 1960s.

Vincent van Gogh: not only did he give us magnificent paintings like *Sunflowers* and *The Yellow House*, he also inspired the song 'Vincent', Don McLean's second-greatest hit after 'American Pie'.

Henri de Toulouse-Lautrec: the short painter who overcame a genetic disability to portray the underbelly of Parisian nightlife like no one managed before or since (to be fair, his view of the can-can was probably also like no one has managed before or since).

Pablo Picasso: mostly famous for his prolific output as a painter, he also turned his creative hands to sculpting, printing, ceramics, poetry, playwriting, stage design and even suspected art theft (when the *Mona Lisa* was stolen from the Louvre in 1911, he was interviewed by police as a suspect).

Jackson Pollock: devised the abstract-expressionist drip-painting style that we can all try our hand at because no one can turn around and say it doesn't look like anything in particular, because it's not supposed to.

Andy Warhol: made art more popular in the 1960s by introducing pop art, which was largely a parody of celebrity culture and mass advertising. Think Campbell's soup and Marilyn Monroe.

Damien Hirst: the versatile artist can turn his hand to many different art forms, but is best known for the sheep, cow and tiger shark he had preserved in formaldehyde.

Banksy: the satirical street art of the anonymous graffiti artist has become famous the world over because it makes people stop and think the world over.

THE BEAUTIFUL MEN OF MUSIC

There are some men who are as famous for their looks as their musical talent. Here are some examples to illustrate the point:

- **Franz Liszt:** while performing in Berlin in 1841, the Hungarian composer was the first musician to have ladies' underwear thrown at him on stage.
- **Elvis Presley:** the King of Rock 'n' Roll unleashed his snake hips on the world in the 1950s and went on to achieve cult status through a combination of great hits and unfeasibly good looks (even if he did get a bit 'portly' towards his untimely early demise).
- **Tom Jones:** referred to as the 'Welsh heartthrob' since the 1960s, he took off where Franz Liszt left off, except this time the underwear had phone numbers on it.
- **David Cassidy:** there were very few teenage girls' bedroom walls that weren't covered in David Cassidy posters in the 1970s.
- **Barry White, aka 'The Walrus of Love':** perhaps not a great beauty, but he had the deep voice every man wants, and he provided evidence that a 'fuller figure' won't stop you fathering a handful of children.
- **Village People:** even if you're not gay, you are every time a DJ puts on 'YMCA' at a wedding or New Year's Eve party (I always wanted to be the cowboy).
- **Boy George:** he took the flamboyant New Romantic look of the 1980s to new heights with his androgynous style.
- **Justin Bieber:** the Canadian singer-songwriter that every mother wanted her daughter to marry so they could both spend more time with him.
- **Harry Styles:** initially famous as a pin-up member of boy band One Direction, he has already gone on to solo success as a singer and actor.

TOUGH TRIVIA

Some trivia can either cause us to tense our muscles in readiness for the next big challenge or make us squirm uncomfortably in our seats. Look through the following and see where they sit on your 'man-o-meter'. Give yourself a point for each muscle-tense and deduct one for each squirm:

In **Antarctica**, the sun rises once at the beginning of summer and sets once at the beginning of winter. This affords 24/7 sunbathing opportunities for six months, although your extremities are unlikely to be intact after the first day.

There are more than 200 corpses on **Mount Everest**, some of which are used as waypoints for climbers.

In **Ancient Rome**, if the script of a play required the death of an actor, a convicted murderer would be sent on in the place of the actor at the last minute. This live execution gave the drama a degree of realism that is difficult to match these days.

Hundreds of people have already died from **'killfies'**, meaning they have killed themselves while concentrating on getting the perfect selfie. Many have fallen to their death from the top of a cliff or high building; others have posed for too long in front of a moving train.

There are vinegar posts on **Australian beaches** because vinegar may be all that stands between you and cardiac arrest if you have been stung by a box jellyfish. It is a myth that urinating on your sting might save you (all it will do is make your death a bit smellier).

KNOWLEDGEABLE QUOTES

YOU CANNOT OPEN A BOOK WITHOUT LEARNING SOMETHING.

Confucius

• • • • • • • • •

THERE IS MUCH PLEASURE TO BE GAINED FROM USELESS KNOWLEDGE.

Bertrand Russell

KNOWLEDGEABLE JOKES

TELL A MAN THERE ARE 300 BILLION STARS IN THE UNIVERSE AND HE WILL BELIEVE YOU. TELL HIM A BENCH HAS WET PAINT ON IT AND HE WILL HAVE TO TOUCH IT TO BE SURE.

• • • • • • • • •

Q: HOW MANY SURREALISTS DOES IT TAKE TO SCREW IN A LIGHT BULB?

A: A FISH.

REALLY USEFUL TRIVIA

Some trivia is only useful for pub quizzes, whereas other trivia can actually be put to good use. Here are a few tips to illustrate the point:

- In **Germany** no one is considered to be legally drunk during Oktoberfest. Go for it.
- It is against the law to urinate in a canal in the **Netherlands** unless you're pregnant (which, if you're reading this book, is fairly unlikely).
- A number of deaths in the **Philippines** have become known as the 'My Way' killings, because they have been perpetrated in karaoke bars by customers who just couldn't stand listening to the song one more time. Maybe just stick to 'Bohemian Rhapsody', even if it is a bit more challenging.
- If you find yourself inside the jaws of a crocodile in **the tropics**, push your thumbs into its eyes and it will let you go immediately (or at least it will let go of what's left of you).

MOVIE MEN TRIVIA

Charlie Chaplin once entered a Charlie Chaplin lookalike competition and failed to reach the final.

Brad Pitt injured his Achilles tendon while playing the part of Achilles in *Troy*, which ironically delayed production by several weeks.

Michael J. Fox's middle name is Andrew.

The Oscar for 'most Academy Awards won by a male' goes to – **Walt Disney** (he won 22 of them).

Woody Harrelson's father was a contract killer.

Jack Nicholson had a runner to polish his axe during filming of *The Shining*. The runner was future pop impresario Simon Cowell.

Johnny Depp suffers from coulrophobia, a fear of clowns.

In 1981, ex-movie actor **Ronald Reagan** became president of the USA. In 1964, he had been turned down for the role of US president in a movie because he wasn't considered to have 'the presidential look'.

MEMORABLE MOVIE MEN

Some men are so cool when they appear on the silver screen that we all want to be just like them. Here are just some of the coolest-ever guys made famous by Hollywood:

Clint Eastwood: after appearing as Rowdy Yates in the hugely successful TV Western series *Rawhide*, Clint Eastwood became famous as the strong, silent drifter in Sergio Leone's spaghetti Westerns and then as don't-mess-with-me cop Harry Callahan in the *Dirty Harry* movies.

Bruce Lee: the actor who kicked his way to fame in a number of 1970s kung fu movies is also credited with popularising martial arts in the West.

Steve McQueen: known by his fans as 'The King of Cool'. Some of his major box-office successes were *Papillon*, *The Magnificent Seven*, *The Great Escape* and *The Towering Inferno*. Posters and clips of his legendary motorcycle scenes on a Triumph TR6 in 1963 in *The Great Escape* remain popular to this day.

Harrison Ford: if you've played Han Solo in the *Star Wars* movies and the action hero in the *Indiana Jones* movies, you're cool. If you fly your own fixed-wing aircraft and helicopters in real life, you're even cooler.

Tom Cruise: his iconic roles include Lieutenant Pete 'Maverick' Mitchell in *Top Gun* and Impossible Mission Force agent Ethan Hunt in the *Mission: Impossible* movies. Even more impressive is the fact that he does a lot of his own stunts at great personal risk.

John Travolta: shot to stardom with his acting and dancing in *Saturday Night Fever* and *Grease* in the 1970s, and two decades later treated us to both again in *Pulp Fiction*. He doesn't just fly his own planes; he has a runway on his Florida property with a taxiway to his house.

Samuel L. Jackson: has appeared in more than a hundred movies and achieved truly iconic status in his collaborations with director Quentin Tarantino, including alongside John Travolta in *Pulp Fiction*. He has enough clout to insist on a clause in his movie contracts that allows him to play golf twice a week.

Jason Statham: carries out many of his own combat routines and stunts because he just happens to be good at kung fu, kickboxing and karate. His iconic antihero roles include Bacon in *Lock, Stock and Two Smoking Barrels*, Frank Martin in the *Transporter* movies and Arthur Bishop in *The Mechanic*.

Daniel Craig: not content with playing British Secret Service agent 007 in the James Bond movies, Daniel Craig also appeared as 007 alongside Queen Elizabeth II at the opening ceremony of the London 2012 Olympic Games. The world watched with open mouths as the two of them parachuted into the Olympic Stadium (although I have long suspected that they used doubles for that).

Idris Elba: with a string of TV and movie hits under his belt, including *The Wire*, *Luther* and the Marvel *Avengers* movies, Elba was voted Sexiest Man Alive 2018 by *People* magazine.

WHEN THE GOING GETS TOUGH...

This book pays homage to many great men on an individual basis, but there are also certain categories of 'hard men' that have made their mark in history:

Pony Express rider: a combination of strength, stamina, fast horsemanship and a willingness to risk death daily, even in the middle of the Paiute War between Native Americans and settlers, were the requirements of the job that got the US Mail from one side of the country to the other. The record crossing took just 7 days and 17 hours in 1860 – to get word of Abraham Lincoln's election in the east to Californian newspapers in the west – and the most famous of the company's despatch riders was Buffalo Bill Cody.

Canadian Mountie: the Royal Canadian Mounted Police began life in the late nineteenth century hunting down illegal whisky traders and policing the Klondike Gold Rush. They were so successful at hunting down criminals over vast distances, usually on horseback or driving a dogsled, that they were often portrayed in the movies under the banner 'the Mountie always gets his man'. A good fact to impress your friends with is that Francis Dickens, son of English author Charles Dickens, served with them between 1874 and 1886.

Samurai: influenced by Zen and Buddhist philosophies, these early Japanese warriors were drawn from the upper reaches of society and had such an influence on military strategy and codes of conduct that their teachings continue to influence everyday life and martial arts in Japan today.

Musketeer: although the King's Musketeers established to guard the French king in the seventeenth century were so called because they were issued with muskets, Hollywood has generally preferred them as swashbuckling swordsmen. Whatever your choice of weapon, though, it rarely payed to mess with them.

Special Forces operative: only the toughest of the toughest were selected for the high-risk, clandestine, commando operations that helped turn the tide in the Allies' favour during World War Two. They included the members of the US Amphibious Scouts and Raiders (since morphed into the US Navy SEALs) and the British SAS (Special Air Service) and SBS (Special Boat Service). These tough guys remain as vital as ever today in the ongoing struggle against terrorism.

Superhero: having their antecedents in fictional yet perfectly human characters like Robin Hood, the Scarlet Pimpernel and Zorro, it was only a matter of time before heroes with superhuman powers evolved. The golden age of comic books in the last century brought us Superman, Captain Marvel, The Flash, Spider-Man, Batman, Hulk, Thor, Wolverine and the X-Men, among many others (including a pantheon of female ones).

KNOW YOUR ROMANS

We all know that Roman emperors and military generals were all-powerful and that they did some pretty weird stuff that usually proved to be their undoing. Here are six of the best to help you remember who undid themselves and how:

Julius Caesar: declared himself dictator for life but then forgot to beware the Ides of March.

Mark Antony: when it came to Cleopatra, he couldn't keep his snake in his trousers and they both ended up having to commit suicide after military defeat.

Caligula: thought he was a god and appointed his horse Incitatus as a priest. He was assassinated after taking sadistic debauchery to a whole new level.

Nero: had his own mother murdered and allegedly fiddled with his lyre while Rome burned. He committed suicide after being condemned to death for being too much of a tyrant.

Hadrian: there was no one better at building walls but he had his lover Antinous declared a god, which is right up there with making your horse a priest. Managed to die of natural causes, a rare feat for a Roman emperor.

Constantine the Great: turned Christian and moved his capital to Byzantium, which he modestly renamed Constantinople (now Istanbul). He left Rome at the mercy of the Visigoths, who promptly sacked it, and that was the end of Ancient Rome.

KNOWLEDGEABLE QUOTES

THE ONLY SOURCE OF KNOWLEDGE IS EXPERIENCE.

Albert Einstein

• • • • • • • • •

LIFE'S TOUGH, BUT IT'S TOUGHER WHEN YOU'RE STUPID.

John Wayne

KNOWLEDGEABLE JOKES

A MAN WALKED INTO A BOOKSTORE AND ASKED THE CLERK: 'CAN YOU DIRECT ME TO THE SELF-HELP SECTION?'

'SURE,' SHE REPLIED, 'BUT WOULDN'T THAT DEFEAT THE PURPOSE?'

• • • • • • • • •

WHY CAN'T YOU TRUST AN ATOM?

BECAUSE THEY MAKE UP LITERALLY EVERYTHING.

UNUSUAL MALE ANIMALS

Some male animals are as famous for their strange characteristics and behaviours as much as anything. Consider the following:

The male **emperor penguin** has to be as hard as nails to stand over the egg it has been charged with incubating for more than 60 days on the inhospitable frozen wastes of Antarctica. It is constantly battered by ice-cold winds and doesn't get as much as a single fish to eat for the whole two months.

The male **seahorse** is unusual within the animal kingdom for incubating the eggs of the female in his pouch until they hatch two to four weeks later and for taking the next batch on board within hours or days.

The **clownfish**, which is always born male, goes even further than the seahorse by changing sex completely, including reproductive organs. This happens each time a dominant female needs replacing at the top of the hierarchical chain.

The Indonesian name for the **proboscis monkey** on the island of Borneo translates as 'Dutchman' because the locals thought that their early Dutch colonisers bore a remarkable resemblance to the weird-looking monkey. The physical traits they were thought to have in common were a large pot belly and a huge, red bulbous nose.

'TIME WAITS FOR NO MAN'

This proverb was adapted into popular usage from English writer Geoffrey Chaucer's original quote in his *Canterbury Tales* that 'time and tide wait for no man', but do you even know which time refuses to wait for you in the twenty-first century? Or which times you should in fact avoid if at all possible? Let me explain.

THE YEAR THAT IS

If, by way of example, you are reading this book sometime in 2019, you are also likely reading it in the following years:

- 1440/41 AH (Islamic year)
- 4717 aka Year of the Pig (Chinese year)
- 5121 Kali Yuga (Hindu year)
- 5779/80 AM (Jewish year)
- 6019 AL (Masonic year)
- 7218 (Age of Earth according to some creationists)

DOG DAYS

If you wondered what Florence and the Machine were on about in their 2009 hit single 'Dog Days Are Over', wonder no more. The dog days run from 3 July to 11 August, which are typically the hottest days of the year in the northern hemisphere. Ancient astrologers put this down to Sirius (the Dog Star) rising and setting in tandem with the sun. Tradition has it that you should avoid medical treatment, overexertion and especially carnal knowledge over the period of the dog days. Even baseball-watching has been known to be avoided, resulting in special dog-day promotions to encourage fans to attend stadiums across North America during this time.

DISMAL DAYS

There are some days on which you should expect to have no fun whatsoever. They were originally identified by Egyptian astrologers as being unlucky and later became known as *dies mali* (evil days), from which the word 'dismal' then derived. The dismal days on which you should avoid getting out of bed if you possibly can are as follows:

- January 1, 25
- February 4, 26
- March 1, 28
- April 10, 20
- May 3, 25
- June 10, 16
- July 13, 22
- August 1, 30
- September 3, 21
- October 3, 22
- November 5, 28
- December 7, 22

Note: we are all aware that Friday the thirteenth is the unluckiest of all days, so when it falls on 13 July, which is also a dismal day, you should definitely head for the hills. Because this happened in 2018, though, it will be 2029 before you have to worry about it again (but worry you should).

A FORCE FOR GOOD

Some men have ended up doing a world of good simply by trying to do the right thing by their fellow human beings. Here are some of the very best:

Mahatma Gandhi: in the face of oppression and brutality on the part of the British Raj, Gandhi secured independence for India in 1947 after years of peaceful protest, non-cooperation and self-deprivation.

Martin Luther King, Jr: the American civil rights leader paved the way to racial equality in the USA with his non-violent opposition to segregation and his famous 'I have a dream' speech on 28 August 1963. He was assassinated in 1968 and the date of his birthday, 15 January, is now celebrated across the USA as Martin Luther King Jr Day.

Nelson Mandela: after 27 years in prison for protesting against South African apartheid, Mandela showed an extraordinary amount of forgiveness when he emerged in 1990 to work for a better future for black and white South Africans alike. He spent five years as the country's first black president, forming a multi-ethnic government to ensure a peaceful transition.

Bob Geldof: in 1984, in order to raise funds to alleviate famine in Ethiopia, the Irish musician of Boomtown Rats fame press-ganged the great and the good of the music industry into forming Band Aid and recording the charity single 'Do They Know It's Christmas?'. It quickly raised £8 million and led on to the 1985 Live Aid concert held simultaneously at Wembley Stadium in London and John F. Kennedy Stadium in Philadelphia. That concert raised a further £150 million.

Bill Gates: the man responsible for the world's personal computer revolution has gone on to establish a charitable foundation with assets of around US$50 billion to reduce extreme poverty and enhance healthcare and education on a global scale.

NOBEL PEACE PRIZE LAUREATES

Martin Luther King, Jr and Nelson Mandela both won the Nobel Peace Prize for their humanitarian efforts. Here is a small selection of other great men who have received that most prestigious of awards:

- 1983: **Lech Wałęsa**, the Polish trade union leader who ultimately achieved free elections for his country and became its president.
- 1989: the fourteenth **Dalai Lama**, in recognition of his Buddhist philosophy and drive for peace and human rights in Tibet.
- 1990: **Mikhail Gorbachev**, the last leader of the Soviet Union, whose policies of *glasnost* (openness) and *perestroika* (restructuring) contributed to the end of the Cold War.
- 2001: **Kofi Annan**, the Ghanaian diplomat who became secretary-general of the United Nations and worked hard to combat HIV.
- 2009: **Barack Obama**, the US president who did much to improve cooperation between nations and introduced liberal reforms in the areas of health, education and LGBT rights.
- 2016: **Juan Manuel Santos**, the Colombian president who finally brought an end to a civil war that had lasted for more than 50 years.

PROPER GENIUSES

There are some men who are so utterly genius that they would be a real inspiration to us if we were only clever enough to follow in their footsteps. Most of us aren't. Here are some such men:

Albert Einstein: best known for his general theory of relativity, one of the pillars of modern physics, and for producing the most famous equation known to man: $E = mc^2$, or energy equals mass times the speed of light squared. The reason for it not being $E = ms^2$ is that he used celeritas, the Latin word for speed, because scientists just do stuff like that sometimes.

Charles Darwin: changed the way humans viewed themselves forever. His work on evolution and natural selection challenged the long-held view that all life was as it was because that is how it had been created by whatever god or gods people believed in.

Louis Pasteur: made our milk safe to drink (and much tastier) by the method still known as pasteurisation in his honour. He also produced the first vaccine against rabies and countless other advances in the treatment of disease.

Alfred Nobel: the man responsible for bequeathing the Nobel Prize to the world was fluent in several languages and a writer of poetry and drama. He was also a chemist and inventor with 355 patents to his name, one of which was for the invention of dynamite.

Stephen Hawking: in spite of the motor neurone disease that afflicted him since the age of 21, Hawking popularised science by explaining difficult concepts in understandable ways. His work on black holes helped confirm the Big Bang theory, because black holes are a bit like the Big Bang in reverse. He even found time to squeeze in guest appearances on *Star Trek: The Next Generation* and *The Simpsons*.

Hiroshi Ishiguro: as director of the Intelligent Robotics Laboratory at Osaka University, Ishiguro has developed lifelike humanoids with facial movements and even has them teach his students sometimes. His robots can process and reply to speech, glance in your direction, blink regularly, shrug their shoulders and even mimic breathing. It's only a matter of time until we can't tell them apart from ourselves (except they'll look and age a lot better than we will).

STUFF THAT CAN DO A MAN'S HEAD IN

There is some stuff that's just too hard to understand, but the following tips will help you bluff your way through any dinner-party conversation:

Once atoms and molecules get together, they become things that we know about, like H_2O (water) and CO_2 (carbon dioxide). If you get stuck with a chemist at a party, always speak in symbols wherever possible. It helps to break the frozen H_2O.

If you need salt at the table, ask someone to pass you sodium and chloride in equal measure. You'll be the talk of the dinner-party circuit with this one, I promise you.

The French word for pie chart is camembert.

Biologists reckon that most component parts of the human body replace themselves on such a regular basis that our body is likely to always be on average less than ten years old.

If you want to lose weight, move to Mars, where you will weigh less than half as much as you do on earth.

If the empty space in atoms could be removed, the entire human race could shrink down to the size of a sugar cube, but the sugar cube would weigh ten times more than all humans currently alive. We are literally a waste of space.

There are more atoms in a teaspoonful of water than there are teaspoonfuls of water in the Atlantic Ocean.

With another five to eight hours' worth being added every minute, it would already take over a thousand years to watch all of the videos on YouTube, so you need to be picky if you don't think you'll live that long or if you have other stuff to do.

Around 12 new books are added to Amazon every hour of every day. This book is one of more than millions now available on Amazon, so you did very well to find it if that's where you bought it and I'm very pleased you did.

Egosurfing is the act of searching the web to see what turns up under your own name.

Googleganger is the name given to a person who turns up with the same name as you when you egosurf. If I google myself, I turn up alongside the entry for the extensive discography of the Ray Hamilton Orchestra and the Ray Hamilton who was sprung from prison by fellow gang members Bonnie and Clyde just before they themselves were gunned down.

FAMOUS LOVERS

Some men, in addition to their fame for other good reasons, have also been famous for their prowess in the bedroom, or for the insatiable and unconditional love they have shown to their partner or partners. Let's admire some of these great romantics:

King Edward I: when Queen Eleanor died in Lincolnshire in 1290, her funeral procession to Westminster Abbey in London took 13 days. Her devoted husband Edward had 12 elaborate crosses erected in her honour, one in each place the procession had stopped overnight.

Shah Jahan: the seventeenth-century Mughal emperor built the Taj Mahal as a shrine to the love of his life, his third wife Mumtaz Mahal. The white-marble Taj Mahal is not just the greatest monument to love that ever was, it also remains one of the world's architectural wonders.

Giacomo Casanova: the name of this eighteenth-century Venetian adventurer became a byword for 'womaniser' following publication of his autobiography, which recounted 122 affairs with women and a fair few 'probables' with men.

King Edward VIII: the man who gave up the British throne in 1936 to marry his American sweetheart Wallis Simpson had to live as an outcast for the rest of his days.

Rudolf Nureyev: the Russian who defected to the West during the Cold War is considered by many to be the best male ballet dancer who ever lived. He was also said to be a loyal friend to his many male and female lovers.

MAN SKILLS

This is an area where many men come into their own. Give them a garden shed, a garage or a workshop to potter about in and they're happy. Give them something to hit and a thing to hit it with and they're even happier. Some of us are better at being practical than others, of course, and some become famous for doing it on a grand scale, like Isambard Kingdom Brunel or Gustave Eiffel, say. In this chapter, we'll take inspiration from these great men and their achievements and then move on to what we can do for ourselves on an infinitely smaller scale.

INSPIRATIONAL ARCHITECTS AND BUILDERS

It takes vision to imagine something truly great on the drawing board, and great skill and determination to see it through to completion no matter what. Here are some of the men who have displayed that rare combination to produce works of genius:

Sir Christopher Wren: the English scientist, mathematician and architect is best remembered for creating dozens of churches after the Great Fire of London in 1666, including the famous St Paul's Cathedral.

Lancelot 'Capability' Brown: considered to be 'England's greatest gardener', Capability Brown designed over 170 large parks in the eighteenth century. It was landscaping on a huge scale and many of his creations can still be admired today.

Baron Haussmann: commissioned by Emperor Napoleon III in 1854 to redesign an overcrowded Paris, the urban renovation that Haussmann achieved over the following 17 years gave the city the harmonious look that it continues to enjoy today.

Frank Lloyd Wright: hailed by many as the greatest American architect of all time, Frank Lloyd Wright designed 'organic' buildings that fitted within their natural environment and took into account the needs and desires of the people who would use them.

Isambard Kingdom Brunel: the acclaimed engineer masterminded the building of dockyards, transatlantic steamships, suspension bridges and the Great Western Railway in the south-west of England.

Gustave Eiffel: the French civil engineer was known as the 'magician of iron'. His masterpieces included the interior structure of the Statue of Liberty, the Maria Pia bridge over the river Douro in Porto and 33 railway locomotives for the Egyptian government. Oh, and some tower in Paris apparently.

Antoni Gaudí: the Spanish architect defied conventional style and favoured curves and waves over straight lines and edges. His most famous work is the Cathedral of the Sagrada Familia in Barcelona, which he worked on from 1883 until his death in 1926. It is such a grand and complex building that it has not yet been finished, but it is hoped that it will be ready for the centenary of his death in 2026.

Frank Gehry: this prolific Canadian–American architect was famous for his avant-garde style and use of unconventional building materials. Some of his creations remain well-known sights today, including the Guggenheim Museum in Bilbao, Spain, the Walt Disney Concert Hall in Los Angeles and the Opus Hong Kong Tower.

Renzo Piano: the Italian architect has given us the Centre Georges Pompidou in Paris, the Shard in London and the rejuvenation of the FIAT factory in Turin (the one with an oval racetrack on the roof).

Norman Foster: the English architect has a CV that includes his work on the restored Reichstag in Berlin, the world's tallest bridge (the Millau Viaduct in France), the HSBC building in Hong Kong, the Apple Campus in California and the Virgin Galactic Spaceport in New Mexico. Perhaps he should think about designing one on the moon for Richard Branson to land his spaceships on.

AWE-INSPIRING STRUCTURES

Man's ingenuity has known no bounds since he figured out how to hew stone and arrange it in a way that might please the gods. He has since moved on to build magnificent structures to serve the latter-day gods of earthly pleasure and aggrandisement. Witness the following examples:

Stonehenge: the 47 stones of the Stonehenge circle in England are Neolithic monuments used thousands of years ago for pagan rituals.

Great Pyramid of Giza: the oldest of the Seven Wonders of the Ancient World, the giant limestone and granite pyramid outside Cairo remains intact more than 4,500 years on.

Great Wall of China: built over thousands of years to protect China from invaders to the north, the fortified wall ended up stretching over 20,921 km (13,000 miles) in an east–west direction.

Chichen Itza: the stepped pyramids of the Mayan civilisation in Mexico might be less famous than the Great Pyramid of Giza, but they are nonetheless well worth seeing.

Colosseum: the iconic oval amphitheatre in Rome is the largest ever built and could hold up to 80,000 spectators to see gladiatorial contests, executions and even mock sea battles.

Taj Mahal: the ivory-white marble and symmetrical Mughal architecture of this mausoleum in Agra, India, combine to create an unsurpassable level of serenity.

Leaning Tower of Pisa: a bit of a cock-up, granted, given that no one noticed the ground was a bit soft on one side before they knocked it up, but the tilt does rather add to the charm of an otherwise stupendous piece of architecture.

Eiffel Tower: Gustave's most famous structure continues to grace Paris 130 years on from the World's Fair it was built for. Looking up at it and looking down from it are equally impressive.

Golden Gate Bridge: the famous suspension bridge looks more red than golden, of course, but it remains San Francisco's most iconic sight. Try to catch it at sunset if you can.

Empire State Building: the art deco masterpiece tapers 443 m (1,453 ft) into the Manhattan skyline and remains one of the great New York sights.

Pyramid at the Louvre: Parisians had to overcome their initial shock at the sight of a glass and steel pyramid erected in the courtyard of the world's most-visited museum, but even they had to admit in the end that it just works.

Sydney Opera House: the design-winning opera house adds interest to Sydney Harbour and combines with the equally impressive Sydney Harbour Bridge to provide one of the world's great settings.

Burj Khalifa: the tiered skyscraper in Dubai has, at 828 m (2,716 ft), been the tallest building in the world since 2008, although it is due to be surpassed in around 2020 by both the Dubai Creek Tower and the Jeddah Tower in Saudi Arabia, which are both aiming to pass the 1 km (3,280 ft) mark.

STATUESQUE STATUES

Sometimes mankind just can't help thinking big, whether driven by their own or someone else's desire to commemorate or worship someone or something. Here are some of the most awe-inspiring statues that you should try to see during your lifetime if you possibly can:

Moai (Easter Island): these monolithic human figures with oversized heads have been mesmerising travellers to Easter Island for centuries. The tallest of the thousand or so statues stands 10 m (33 ft) high.

Great Sphinx of Giza (Cairo): this limestone statue of a mythical creature with a lion's body and a man's head stands on the west bank of the Nile close to the Pyramids of Giza. It is the oldest and largest monolith in the world.

Terracotta Army (Xian): the 8,000 soldiers, 130 chariots and 670 horses of the Terracotta Army were created to protect the first emperor of China, Qin Shi Huang, in the afterlife. They are an astonishing sight to behold now and would have been even more astonishing painted in their original bright pigments in 210 BCE.

Statue of David (Florence): Michelangelo's masterpiece in marble stands 5 m (16 ft) tall in the Galleria dell'Accademia in Florence, although there is an exact replica in the Piazza della Signoria if you can't get into the museum (try to book in advance if you can).

Statue of Liberty (New York): situated on Liberty Island off Manhattan, the iconic statue was a gift from France in 1886 to commemorate the centenary of the Declaration of Independence (the ten-year delay was down to difficulty in securing funds on both sides of the Atlantic).

Christ the Redeemer (Rio de Janeiro): the largest art deco statue in the world at 30 m (98 ft), it looms much larger because the outstretched arms of Christ span 28 m (92 ft) and the statue is sited on top of the 700-m (2,296-ft) Corcovado mountain.

The Thinker: this monumental bronze sculpture by Auguste Rodin is of a male resting his chin on his hand while deep in thought about something or other. It can be seen at the Musée Rodin in Paris.

The Motherland Calls (Volgograd): the largest non-religious statue in the world at 85 m (279 ft), the giant figure of a woman holding aloft a sword commemorates the brutal Battle of Stalingrad in World War Two.

Giant Buddhas: the three largest statues in the world were all of buddhas until the Statue of Unity was completed in India in 2018 (see below). The Buddhas are Ushiku Daibutsu in Japan at 120 m (394 ft); Laykyun Setkyar in Myanmar at 130 m (426 ft); and Spring Temple Buddha in China at 153 m (502 ft). The Spring Temple Buddha was built in remembrance of the earlier Bamiyan Buddhas blown up in Afghanistan by the Taliban.

Statue of Unity: now the highest statue in the world at 183 m (600 ft), the Statue of Unity in Gujarat depicts and is dedicated to the Indian independence leader Vallabhbhai Patel. It is surrounded by a huge artificial lake.

SKILFUL QUOTES

ARCHITECTURE IS THE THOUGHTFUL MAKING OF SPACE.

Louis Kahn

• • • • • • • • •

IT TAKES HALF YOUR LIFE BEFORE YOU DISCOVER THAT LIFE IS A DO-IT-YOURSELF PROJECT.

Napoleon Hill

SKILFUL JOKES

I ASKED OUR NEW BUILDER TO DO SOME ODD JOBS FOR ME. I GAVE HIM A LIST OF TEN, BUT HE ONLY COMPLETED NUMBERS 1, 3, 5, 7 AND 9.

• • • • • • • • • •

I DIDN'T WANT TO ADMIT MY DAD WAS A CONSTRUCTION-SITE THIEF, BUT WHEN I GOT HOME ALL THE SIGNS WERE THERE.

ICONIC TRANSPORT

Some men have put their minds to building large, beautiful things that also serve to move the human race along at ever-faster speeds and in ever-increasing luxury. Here's a reminder of some of man's great accomplishments in the field of transport:

RMS *Titanic*: the largest ship in the world when it was launched in Belfast in 1912. It boasted a grand staircase, Turkish baths, a gymnasium, a Parisian cafe and the ultimate in luxury in its first-class staterooms. Anyway, I'm going to stop there because I don't want to spoil the ending if you haven't seen the movie.

MS *Quantum of the Seas*: the most technologically advanced cruise ship ever to set sail when it was launched in 2014, it offers its passengers an on-board virtual skydiving experience, a surf simulator, an indoor ice rink, a rock-climbing wall and an elevated glass pod providing 360-degree views of the open ocean.

***Flying Scotsman*:** the steam locomotive was the most famous train in the world after setting world records for speed and non-stop distance. It even starred in its own thriller movie in 1929. Retired in 1963, it made 'farewell tours' of North America and Australia before undergoing a series of overhauls which have allowed it to re-enter service running luxury rail trips on British main lines.

20th Century Limited: the iconic Pullman carriages of this luxury service between New York and Chicago were initially hauled back and forth by streamlined, art deco steam locomotives built by Alco (American Locomotive Company). In the 1940s they were replaced by equally iconic General Motors 'bulldog-nosed' diesels, one of which starred in the 1959 Hitchcock spy thriller *North by Northwest*, featuring Cary Grant as 'regular guy on train mistaken for spy'.

Concorde: the world's first supersonic airliner when it took off in 1976. Its adjustable nose allowed maximum streamlining when straightened up during flight and gave the crew visibility for take-off and landing when tilted down. In 1996, it achieved a record time of 2 hours 52 minutes 59 seconds from New York to London.

Boeing 737: not included because it's the biggest or best aircraft ever made, but because it's the most-produced airplane in history. Over 10,000 of the narrow-bodied, short-range jets have been delivered to customers around the world and an average of 1,250 are in the air at any one time.

Chevy Corvette (1963): the '63 Corvette remains to many the pinnacle of American car-building, not least because of its space-age split rear window. Prince enhanced its reputation with his first hit single, 'Little Red Corvette', but it wasn't so little really – it needed a very long chassis to house its huge, throaty V8 engine.

Aston Martin DB5: a 1960s British icon which achieved superstar status as the James Bond car in the 1964 movie *Goldfinger*. Sean Connery was at the controls, which included machine guns and an ejector seat, neither of which came as standard for Aston Martin's regular customers. The DB, rather unexcitingly, stands for David Brown, the owner of Aston Martin at the time.

HANDY DIY TIPS

Back in the land of us mere mortals, houses, cars and gardens still need to be maintained. There are countless books and TV programmes to tell us how to go about it all, but there's no harm in sharing a few tips as we go. So here are mine:

HOUSEHOLD TIPS

Create a workspace that has the following attributes:

- Sufficient space, ventilation and light.
- Large entrance, with sliding doors if possible.
- Opening windows to let out dust.
- A hardwood workbench fitted with vices.
- Separate areas for tasks such as sawing and painting.
- Plenty of storage shelves and hooks to hang tools on.

Spend at least twice as much time stripping/sanding/priming as you do painting or wallpapering. If you don't do the correct preparation, you won't get a nice finish.

If you don't have time to do a job properly, get someone else in to do it for you or at least to help you with it. Fathers and big brothers are especially cheap.

Always hold a nail in place with a clothes peg or a pair of pliers to reduce the risk of smashing your thumb when you swing at it.

Rubbing a walnut on wooden furniture will remove marks and scrapes.

Stretch a rubber band around an open paint tin (i.e. across the open top and under the bottom of the tin to secure it tightly) so that you can wipe excess paint off your brush on the rubber band without getting any paint around the rim of the tin.

Whenever you need to take something apart, lay the pieces out in the order you remove them so that you know how to reassemble them later. Even better, use your phone to take a photo prior to the removal of each piece.

Always turn off the main water valve at your stopcock before messing about with your plumbing.

Always keep the name and number of a plumber handy in case you get a leak or problem you don't know how to fix.

HOUSE-SELLING TIPS

If you want to sell your house, bear the following tips in mind:

Declutter to create the illusion of a larger living space. You can do this by putting some furniture into storage temporarily and by weeding out stuff you really don't need – taking it to the dump will do, but taking it to a charity shop will make you feel better about yourself and improve somebody else's life.

Replace wall paintings with large mirrors to effectively double the size of your rooms.

Touch up shabby paintwork and clean your carpets.

Depending on the season, make sure your home is warm or airy enough to receive potential buyers. The smell of coffee and some low music will also make them feel like they would be happy living in your home.

GARDENING TIPS

Never mow the lawn wet as you will only cut it up.

Always mow your lawn round the perimeter first to create the space you need to turn around when you then mow back and forth in (slightly overlapping) strips.

Finish the lawn off with a roller to create light and dark strips, either at a 90-degree or 45-degree angle from the house.

Use pencil and paper to plan very roughly what you're going to plant where in your garden. You'll then know whether or not it's going to work before you start. Don't go into too much detail, though, or you'll end up with a 'gardening by numbers' look.

Always take account of the soil, light and shade in your garden when deciding what to plant where.

If you're new to gardening, start with plants, flowers and produce that grow more easily than others. Easy-to-grow vegetables include tomatoes, peppers, onions and basil. Easy-to-grow flowers include dahlias, foxgloves, roses, sunflowers, petunias and black-eyed Susans. If you want to get something climbing quickly, go for clematis.

If you're pushed for time or space, consider a 'container garden', e.g. by keeping pot plants on your patio, terrace or balcony. Not only are they easier to maintain than a well-stocked garden, they can also be moved around to follow the sun if needs be during the day and they can be brought into a shed or garage for the winter. They are also much easier for a family member or neighbour to water while you're on holiday.

HACK YOUR CAR INTO STARTING

Jump-starting is a trick every vehicle owner should know how to execute, because it's one of the few things you shouldn't need a garage mechanic or a breakdown guy to do for you. If you're in a residential area, it might well be quicker to ask a kindly stranger to give you a hand to jump-start your dead car by placing their working car alongside yours and opening their bonnet.

Here is the order in which you should attach the red and black leads to the respective cars:

- One red lead on dead car's positive battery terminal.
- Other red lead on donor car's positive battery terminal.
- One black lead on donor car's negative battery terminal.
- Other black lead on something metal (such as the bonnet).
- Start the donor car, then start the dead car.
- If both cars start, remove the four leads in reverse order.
- Thank the owner of the donor car.
- Drive away.

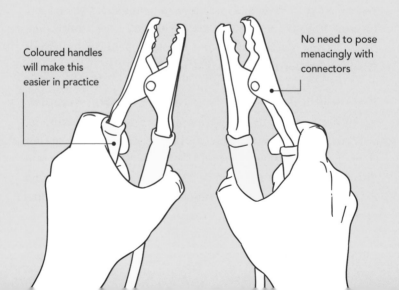

Coloured handles will make this easier in practice

No need to pose menacingly with connectors

HACK THE CRACK IN
YOUR WINDSCREEN

A chip in your windscreen could develop into something more serious, so be sure to do a running repair until you can get it looked at properly.

Nail varnish is the answer, but make sure it's clear nail varnish. Painting a thin layer of it on to the chip – inside and out – will reinforce it and give you some peace of mind. If you don't have nail varnish, a nearby woman might, or you can buy it cheaply from the nearest pharmacy.

You'll need a steady hand!

Window chip, now glazed

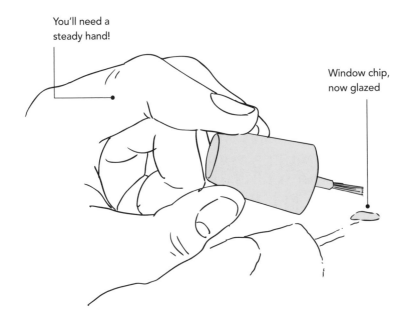

SKILFUL QUOTES

WHEN YOU WANT TO KNOW HOW THINGS REALLY WORK, STUDY THEM WHEN THEY'RE COMING APART.

William Gibson

• • • • • • • • •

AVOID ANYTHING MADE BY AN ENGINEER WHO DOESN'T HAVE ALL HIS OWN FINGERS.

Simon R. Green

SKILFUL JOKES

I'M DEDICATING THIS SHOW
TO MY DAD, WHO WAS A ROOFER.
SO DAD, IF YOU'RE UP THERE...

• • • • • • • •

THE CARPENTER CAME ROUND THE
OTHER DAY. HE MADE THE BEST
ENTRANCE I'VE EVER SEEN.

• • • • • • • •

A CEMENT MIXER COLLIDED WITH
A PRISON VAN. MOTORISTS HAVE
BEEN ASKED TO LOOK OUT FOR
TEN HARDENED CRIMINALS.

PRACTICAL TRIVIA

Here are a few facts that highlight man's vision, ingenuity and determination:

- It is taking longer to build the Cathedral of the Sagrada Familia in Barcelona than it took to build the pyramids in Egypt.
- The two longest bridges in the world are both on the Jinghu High-Speed Railway that runs between Beijing and Shanghai. They are the Danyang–Kunshan Grand Bridge at 164 km (102 miles) and the Langfang–Qingxian viaduct at 114 km (71 miles).
- The world's longest railway tunnel is the 56-km (35-mile) Gotthard Base Tunnel under the Swiss Alps between northern and southern Europe.
- The longest glass-bottomed skywalk is in Chongqing, China. If you hold your nerve, you can walk for 175 m (574 ft) while trying not to look at the ground 123 m (403 ft) below your feet.
- The narrowest house in the world is Keret House in Warsaw. Its width is 91 cm (3 ft) at its narrowest and 1.5 m (5 ft) at its widest. It has a bedroom, kitchen and bathroom over two floors connected by a ladder.

HOW TO DO STUFF PROPERLY

There's some stuff that we men are traditionally very bad at, so here are some tips that will make you look like you know what you're doing:

HOW TO WRAP A GIFT

If there's one thing that men are not always great at, it's wrapping gifts. Here's how to look like you meant it.

- If the present is an awkward shape, buy a box or other container to put it in before you wrap it. If it's a nice box that will come in useful later to the recipient, you'll get extra kudos.
- Remove any price tags.
- Buy the best wrapping paper you can. It doesn't even matter if it costs as much as the present itself. Presentation matters.
- Cut the paper to size and lay the gift face down on it.
- Wrap the paper around the gift and tape the two sides together.
- At both ends, fold the outer edges in like triangles and then fold the whole edge over and tape it.
- Now that the gift is secure in its expensive wrapping paper, add the finishing touches. Ribbon is good and a hand-written gift tag is essential (take as long as you need to think of something appropriate to say on the card, especially if you would quite like to spend the rest of your life with the recipient of the gift).

HOW TO SHOP FOR YOUR PARTNER

Man up and get into some proper shops to choose presents for the love of your life. The shop assistants will soon come running over to help you out. If you really can't face that, set aside enough time to shop online well in advance of the date the present is needed for. Either way, bear the following tips in mind:

- Know your partner's sizes or keep a note of them on your phone. If you're squeamish about rummaging through their wardrobe and drawers to get the information, just ask!
- If your partner ever got a colour chart done, keep a photo of it in your phone.
- Presents that you have put some thought into will be appreciated more than anything, so pay attention to their likes and dislikes and take note of what draws their attention when you're out shopping or watching TV.
- If you're not long into the relationship, ask their family members or friends for ideas.
- Buy anniversary presents that are traditionally appropriate for the anniversary in question, which you can easily check out online.

Note: always remember to update your notes if your partner changes size or if you change your partner.

HOW TO REMEMBER YOUR ANNIVERSARY

Try to get married on your own birthday. Not only will you be able to remember your anniversary every year, you'll be the centre of attention and get lots of presents. Failing that, put an annual alert in your phone, or, if you need a bit more time to get that special present organised, try to plot the date against something more meaningful to you than your anniversary. Here are some suggestions:

- It's always in the week leading up to the Super Bowl.
- It's always in the week following the Masters golf tournament at Augusta.
- It's always during the Wimbledon tennis fortnight.
- It's always exactly two weeks after Facebook sends you a memory of your stag/bachelor party.

Note: never plot the date of your anniversary against the Olympic Games, because, at best, you'll only remember the date once every four years.

HOW TO CHANGE A NAPPY

If you're lucky enough to be a dad, this will be inevitable, so you might as well get used to the idea and get your hand in, so to speak, at the earliest opportunity. Here goes:

- Scrub your hands with soap and water.
- Lie the miniature person on their back and talk rubbish to them.
- Take a deep breath and hold it in.
- Remove the miniature person's outer clothing and unfasten the nappy.
- Suppress your gag reflex.
- Gently wipe the offending area with wet wipes or cotton wool and water.
- Put the wet wipes/cotton wool inside the dirty nappy and seal the whole thing up for early disposal.
- Lifting the miniature person by the ankles with one hand, slide the new nappy into position with the other. Then fold the flap up between the legs. If it's a male miniature person you're dealing with, remember to point Wee Willie Winkie down the way.
- Close with the stretchy tabs and reinstate the miniature person's outer clothing.
- Start breathing again and congratulate yourself on a job well done.
- Tell everyone you know how it went without sparing a single detail about the contents of the nappy. That way, they'll know you're a real dad and no mistaking.

Note: if the baby wasn't yours and you just borrowed it to see what changing a nappy is like, don't forget to give it back. Along with the soiled nappy.

HOW TO WEAR A BABY CARRIER

Even manlier than pushing a pram, a baby carrier also leaves your hands free for other things, like wielding a hammer maybe. Here's how it's done:

- Sponge and scrape off the dribbles and puke from the last time the baby carrier was used.
- Untangle the spaghetti of harnesses that are apparently needed to secure a really small person.
- Climb into the harness, preferably with the help of at least two other adults.
- Insert the small person.
- Face them towards you if their head still wobbles all over the place; face them away from you when their head has steadied down a bit, which also has the advantage of directing any puke into the street.

Note: Daniel Craig – that's right, 007 Secret Agent James Bond – has been spotted carrying his own child in a baby carrier. So if anyone laughs at you for doing it, just chase them over some rooftops, engage them in a high-speed car chase and drop them into shark-infested waters from a moving helicopter. Serves them bloody right. Oh, and don't forget to check that the baby is still in the carrier.

BOYS AND THEIR TOYS

Some men have just had fun messing about with gadgets and machines; others have invented things that changed the world forever. We will look at some of these men and their inventions in this chapter, from Isaac Newton to Nikola Tesla, but starting with the man who could turn his hand to pretty much anything, Leonardo da Vinci. We will also look at what's hot now, from bicycles to cars, from drones to private jets, from cool music players to that most modern of inventions, the digital assistant.

→ LEONARDO DA VINCI ←

The Italian master Leonardo da Vinci was probably the most talented and versatile man who ever graced this earth. Not content with producing the *Mona Lisa* and *The Last Supper*, two of the world's most famous paintings, he was also an inventor, scientist, mathematician, engineer, writer, musician and many other things besides. Here is a tiny fraction of what he turned his hand and mind to:

- Invented the concepts of the parachute, helicopter and tank.

- Combined mathematics and art to produce *Vitruvian Man*, a perfectly proportioned portrayal of the male body (see the Manly Health and Happiness chapter for various tips on how to achieve those perfect proportions).

- He sometimes wrote backwards, presumably to keep his work secret, so you need a mirror to read a lot of what he wrote.

- His dissections of human muscles, nerves and vessels led him to document the mechanics of how we move, and he exposed the nonsense that humans thought with their hearts and not their brains.

- Engineered a system of mobile barricades to protect Venice from attack.

- Designed a bridge in 1502 to cross the Bosporus Strait in Turkey that no one had the nerve to build, but the same design was used to build a bridge in Norway in 2001.

Note: in defence of twenty-first-century man, da Vinci did not have the distractions of email, social media and box sets to contend with, and he was probably rubbish at mixing beer cocktails.

WORLD-CHANGING INVENTORS

Some men are so good at pottering about in their sheds they invent things that make the world a better place forever:

Isaac Newton: in 1687, the English physicist and mathematician came up with the laws of motion, which explained the scale and speed of everything from everyday life to planetary motion. He also developed the first practical telescope and the first coins to be designed and produced with anti-counterfeit measures.

James Watt: in 1781, the Scottish mechanical engineer and chemist produced the first efficient steam engine, which revolutionised industry. He introduced the concept of horsepower and the measurement of electrical and mechanical power is named in his honour, as in 100-watt light bulb.

Alessandro Volta: the Italian physicist and chemist invented the electric battery and continuous electric current, and also discovered methane. His name is immortalised in the volt unit of measurement and therefore remains stamped on millions of batteries around the world to this day.

Benjamin Franklin: this Founding Father of the United States was a veritable polymath. His inventions included the lightning rod, bifocal spectacles and the Franklin stove, and he founded Philadelphia's first fire department and the University of Pennsylvania. He also put in stints as US ambassador to Sweden and France.

Samuel Morse: an accomplished and prolific painter in the first half of his life, he must have surprised a few people in 1837 when he invented the Morse code, the forerunner of communication systems that have kept air transport and shipping safe for nearly 200 years.

Michael Faraday: the Englishman was such an influential scientist that Einstein kept a picture of him on his wall for inspiration. His discoveries in the fields of electricity, magnetism, optics and gases resulted in many practical innovations and improvements to electric power, refrigeration and lighthouses.

George Westinghouse: the American engineer made rail travel much safer when he invented the air brake in 1868. Before then, brakesmen had to run through or along the top of each car in order to apply individual brakes manually.

Thomas Edison: hailed as America's greatest inventor with more than a thousand patents, he is remembered mostly for producing the electric light bulb in America. He also played a major part in the invention of the telegraph, phonograph and motion picture camera, and he did much to establish research labs and mass-production principles on an industrial scale.

Nikola Tesla: the Serbian-American did much to progress the early electric power industry in the late nineteenth century with his many experimental inventions and he was a great showman when he came to demonstrate them. He fell into relative obscurity until the Tesla car and energy company was named after him in 2003 and David Bowie played him in the 2006 movie *The Prestige*.

Alan Turing: the English genius had laid the foundations for the electric computer before he set about breaking the German Enigma code during World War Two, a feat which is said to have shortened the war by several years and thereby saved millions of lives.

GREAT INVENTIONS THROUGH THE AGES

Just to keep everything we take for granted today in some sort of perspective, here is a timeline of some of the major inventions throughout history. It's important to know that there were no tablet computers in the world before 2010, but also that you could get a nice set of wheels in 3500 BC.

Alcohol (7000 BC): it was the Chinese who got the party started.

Wheel (3500 BC): the potters of Mesopotamia were the first guys to get a nice set of wheels.

Compass (206 BC): the Chinese again (they probably needed it to find their way home after all that boozing).

Printing press (1439): good old Johannes Gutenberg ultimately enabled books just like this one.

Bicycle (1817): the dandy horse invented in Germany by Karl Drais may have lacked pedals, but it most certainly paved the way for the cool bicycles we enjoy today.

Steam train (1804): when Englishman Richard Trevithick produced a steam locomotive that shot along the track at a revolutionary 3.8 kph (2.4 mph), he probably didn't see it as the forerunner of 600-kph (374-mph) magnetic levitation trains in the twenty-first century. But it was.

Canned food (1810): Nicolas Appert was the French inventor of the process to seal food in jars and cans. Without this invention, just how many of us would have starved to death in our bachelor pads?

Computer programme (1822): the first programmable machine was invented by English mathematician and engineer Charles Babbage.

Lawnmower (1830): the push mower was invented in England by Edwin Budding because people were fed up with the time it took to cut sports grounds and large gardens with a scythe. Get yourself a John Deere Lawn Tractor to cut that time down even more.

Telephone (1876): the Scottish-American Alexander Graham Bell turned electricity into sound and patented the telephone. It might have been rudimentary compared with today's smartphones, but it worked.

Combustion-engine motor cars (1876–85): German engineering led to the first combustion engine (Nikolaus Otto), four-stroke diesel engine (Rudolf Diesel) and petrol-driven production automobile (Karl Benz).

Phonograph (1877): Thomas Edison came up with the first working phonograph, which led to the gramophone, record player, tape deck, CD player, MP3 downloads and superfast music streaming.

Electric bulb (1879): Joseph Swan and Thomas Edison were granted patents for the incandescent light bulb on opposite sides of the Atlantic. The future was suddenly much clearer.

Zipper (1891): the zip or zipper invented in the USA by Whitcomb Judson allowed men to whip in and out of their trousers (or pants, as Whitcomb would have said) with hitherto unknown speed.

Aircraft (1903): Orville and Wilbur Wright achieved the power of flight at Kitty Hawk, North Carolina. They were airborne for all of 12 seconds and 36 m (120 ft), but manned flight most definitely got off the ground that day.

Domestic refrigerator (1915): it kept the beer cool, granted, but it was another 20 years before fridges also made ice to go in our gin.

Television (1927): Scottish engineer John Logie Baird demonstrated the first working television over a long distance and went on to invent colour television and the electric picture tube, all of which probably makes him the great-grandfather of Netflix.

Jet engine (1944): former Royal Air Force pilot Frank Whittle developed the engine that allowed planes to fly at higher altitudes over longer distances.

Email (1971): the first ever email was sent from one rudimentary computer to another by computer engineer Ray Tomlinson in Cambridge, Massachusetts. Tomlinson's other claim to fame is that he introduced the @ sign as the locator in email addresses.

Personal computer (1975): the MITS (Micro Instrumentation and Telemetry Systems) Altair 8800 started the PC revolution, but Microsoft and Apple were not far behind.

Home video game console (1972): the *Magnavox Odyssey* game lacked colour and sound, but it did lead the way to the Xbox, Sony PlayStation and Nintendo Switch.

Laptop/notebook (1981): Osborne Computers produced the first laptop, followed by IBM, Compaq and NEC. The NEC UltraLite in 1989 was the first laptop which wasn't too heavy to sit on top of your lap.

Internet (1990): English computer engineer Tim Berners-Lee invented the World Wide Web after picking up a basic knowledge of electronics through tinkering with his model railway as a young boy.

Smartphone (1994): the first practical smartphone was the IBM Simon. It was the size of a brick, but it was also the start of a technical revolution. The first iPhone didn't come out until 2007, but it was a game changer alright.

Hybrid car (1997): the Toyota Prius was the first mass-produced gasoline-electric hybrid car.

All-electric car (2008): the first all-electric car produced in significant numbers was the Tesla Roadster. Its lithium-ion battery allowed it to travel 322 km (200 miles) on each charge.

Computer tablet (2010): following some decent earlier attempts by GRiD Systems, IBM, AT&T and Apple, the iPad came out in 2010 to critical acclaim and widespread popularity.

INVENTIVE QUOTES

IF I HAVE SEEN FURTHER, IT IS BY STANDING ON THE SHOULDERS OF GIANTS.

Isaac Newton

• • • • • • • • • •

THE TROUBLE WITH QUOTES FROM THE INTERNET IS THAT IT IS DIFFICULT TO DETERMINE WHETHER OR NOT THEY ARE TRUE.

Abraham Lincoln

INVENTIVE JOKES

THERE ARE TEN TYPES OF PEOPLE IN
THE WORLD: THOSE WHO UNDERSTAND
BINARY, AND THOSE WHO DON'T.

· · · · · · · · ·

THE GUY WHO INVENTED AUTOCORRECT
DIED TODAY. RESTAURANT IN PEACE.

MODERN
TECHNOLOGICAL WIZARDS

Some men spend the carefree days of their youth getting all geeky with their computers. Very few of them go on to change the world forever, but some of them do. Some do it with hardware, some with software. Some do it with both, like Bill Gates and Steve Jobs. Here is a small selection of the greatest technological minds of our time:

Bill Gates: the Microsoft Corporation founded by Bill Gates in 1975 remains the world's largest supplier of personal computers, software and electronics, including its flagship Microsoft Office suite and Xbox game consoles.

Steve Jobs: the Apple company he founded with Steve Wozniak and Ronald Wayne in 1976 probably remains the coolest thing in technology worldwide, providing everything from computers, laptops, tablets and smartphones to music, video, apps and gadgets to meet your every need. It is the world's most valuable brand and even the address of its HQ is pretty cool: Apple Campus, One Infinite Loop, Cupertino, California.

Jeff Bezos: since Amazon was founded by Jeff Bezos from his garage in 1994 as an online bookstore, it has grown to provide just about anything to its some 250 million active users. It is currently the largest Internet-based retailer in the USA and many other countries where it has a presence.

Pierre Omidyar: the French-born American computer scientist was responsible for the launch of the eBay consumer-to-consumer and business-to-consumer auction site, which has since expanded to provide 'buy it now' shopping alongside online auctions in more than 30 countries. Who says the French don't have a word for entrepreneur?

Mark Zuckerberg: launched Facebook on his college campus at Harvard in 2004. Within three years it had been made available to everyone in the world over the age of 13 with a valid email address. Now it has over 1.6 billion active users. The story behind the creation of Facebook has been captured in the 2010 movie *The Social Network* starring Jesse Eisenberg (as Zuckerberg), Andrew Garfield (as scorned alleged co-creator) and Justin Timberlake (as the founder of Napster).

Jack Dorsey: the first ever tweet on Twitter was sent by the network's co-founder Jack Dorsey in 2006. It read 'just setting up my twttr'. Now about 500 million tweets are posted each day by around 300 million users, making it second only to Facebook in popularity. The words posted in Twitter feeds each day would fill a ten-million-page book.

Gary Kremen: Internet dating sites have become big business accommodating every flavour and age of would-be dater and have resulted in many relationships and marriages that could never otherwise have happened. But beware – the founder of Match.com, Gary Kremen, lost his girlfriend to a man she found on Match.com.

NEW TOYS ON THE BLOCK

Every year we have newer and better toys to play with. Here are some of the things that came to the fore in the past couple of years alone:

Leatherman Tread LT: this 'mangle' (man bangle) comes with 29 tools and still manages to look great on your wrist (in a Mad Max kind of way). If you can't live with the raw mangle, just upgrade by paying more for the Leatherman Tempo Watch attachment to make it look more 'watchy'.

Amazon Key: a kit that allows delivery drivers to access a customer's home (and sometimes car) for the purpose of delivering goods. The kit contains a smart door lock with one-use password capability and a camera to record each delivery.

GoPro Fusion: this top-of-the-range, waterproof action camera will set you back a bit, but it will capture 360-degree video with surround sound and it can be voice-controlled when you need to keep your hands free. You can even link it to a Karma drone for aerial shots.

B&O BeoSound 2 speakers: these 360-degree, wireless, Dalek-like smart speakers have Google Assistant built in and truly look and sound the part.

Shazam: one of the ten most popular apps in the world, Shazam can identify pretty much any piece of music, movie, TV show or advert if you play it a clip. And it's free.

Monty Digital Radio by VQ: the Scandi retro look of this radio belies its full-range, ultra-wide sound. Operates as a Bluetooth speaker as well as a radio.

Brompton Electric bicycle: these hugely popular folding bikes have just moved up a gear with 250-watt motors and a custom-built battery pack designed with the help of the Williams F1 racing team. Navigating city streets is easy and you don't have to change out of Lycra when you reach the office. They cost considerably more than the solely human-powered version, but they will flatten hills for you.

iPhone XS: the sharpest display of any phone ever, but the iPhone 8 is just as quick if budget is an issue. If Android is your thing, it's hard to beat the Samsung Galaxy S9 Plus and its excellent camera.

Video gaming: *Red Dead Redemption 2* and *Death Stranding* are two of the hottest video games released in recent times. *Red Dead Redemption 2* is the continuing story of outlaw Arthur Morgan in the Wild West. *Death Stranding* is an action game that straddles life and death and 'stars' Norman Reedus (of *The Walking Dead* fame), Mads Mikkelsen (the coolest Scandi actor ever) and Léa Seydoux (the French actress who starred as a Bond girl in *Spectre*).

Bombardier Global 7500: the world's largest and longest-range private jet has four sitting areas with armchairs, sofas and flat-screen TVs, plus an en suite shower in the Master Suite. Meals are prepared fresh in the on-board full-size kitchen. If you have to ask the price, you can't afford it. (It's about US$75 million.)

A GOOD HACK TO AVOID BEING HACKED

With so many different devices, accounts and apps demanding passwords from us, and insisting that we change them on a regular basis and don't write them down, we simply have no way of remembering them all. Or have we?

One way is to check them out under 'Website and App Passwords' within 'Settings' if you have that facility on your device. Another is to install one of the many 'password manager' applications that will encrypt, store and retrieve your passwords for you.

Perhaps the best trick, though, is to set up passwords that are memorable in the first place, such as an easy-to-remember acronym. For example, I might use #m34dliA! knowing full well that it stands for '#my 34-year-old daughter lives in Australia!' Note that this acronym contains a mixture of upper- and lower-case characters plus two symbols and two numbers, a combination that considerably strengthens your password.

HACK YOUR WAY OUT OF TROUBLE

Never go anywhere without your essential multitool in your pocket, glove compartment or rucksack, whether it be a Swiss Army knife, a Leatherman or any other tried-and-tested brand. Then, the next time you find yourself in trouble in the great outdoors, or a damsel or fellow man in distress asks if you can help to fix, tighten, loosen, uncork or repair something, you can just whip out your multitool and choose from the following parts to get the job done:

- Screwdrivers (small, medium, large and Phillips)
- Knives (small, medium)
- Pliers
- Wire cutters, stripper and crimper
- Miniature saws (metal, wood)
- Punch
- Cleaning rod
- Awl
- Ruler
- Can opener
- Bottle opener
- Corkscrew
- Scissors
- LED light
- Magnifying lens

In 2006, Wenger brought out a Swiss Army knife called 'The Giant', which retailed at around US$1,000. It had 87 tools with 141 different functions and was recognised by Guinness World Records as the World's Most Multifunctional Penknife.

Note: the one place you shouldn't take your multitool is through airport security – that's asking for trouble.

INVENTIVE QUOTES

TECHNOLOGY IS ANYTHING THAT WASN'T AROUND WHEN YOU WERE BORN.

Alan Kay

· · · · · · · · ·

IF WE WORKED ON THE ASSUMPTION THAT WHAT IS ACCEPTED AS TRUE REALLY IS TRUE, THERE WOULD BE LITTLE HOPE FOR ADVANCE.

Orville and Wilbur Wright

INVENTIVE JOKES

MY EMAIL PASSWORD HAS BEEN
HACKED. THAT'S THE FOURTH TIME
I'VE HAD TO RENAME THE CAT.

• • • • • • • • •

THE ONLY DIFFERENCE BETWEEN BOYS
AND MEN IS THE PRICE OF THEIR TOYS.

COOL WHEELS

So many to choose from, but here are some that have not been coming off the production line for long:

BMW i8 Roadster: BMW's top-of-the-range, open-top version of its hybrid supercar is sleek and almost silent. It has increased power and driving range over the previous model, and a roof that slips down in 14 seconds.

Tesla Model S: if you aren't bothered about having a convertible, look at the futuristic Tesla Model S, which has an electric range of 400–540 km (250–335 miles), or the Tesla Model 3, the world's first affordable luxury all-electric car.

Lamborghini Urus: if you've always dreamed of a beautiful, Italian-designed SUV, the Lamborghini Urus can be yours for a small fortune. Or you can go for the even newer Alfa Romeo Stelvio SUV for a lot less money.

Two of the hottest cars to look out for from 2019 onwards are the **Aston Martin Varekai** and the **Bentley Barnato**.

If two wheels are more your thing, have a look at the two new Bobbers on the block. The (American) **Indian Scout Bobber** and the (British) **Triumph Bonneville Bobber** are both low-riding, blacked-out cruisers that somehow look retro and freshly custom-built at the same time. There's nothing between them in price or performance, so it's all a matter of personal preference on the looks (which aren't all that different either).

THE DRONE

When it comes to boys and their toys, drone technology has caused as much excitement as anything in recent years, whether for civil or military purposes. Unmanned aerial vehicles (UAVs), to give them their proper title, were first used as target practice for warships as long ago as World War One, before developing into sophisticated military surveillance and hunter-killer systems. As with many gadgets originally developed by the military, the technology has since spread into other areas, including the following:

- Aerial photography and videos, including for movie shoots, holiday snaps and weddings
- Product and postal deliveries
- Disaster relief, including delivery of food and medical supplies
- Search and rescue
- Policing
- Bomb disposal
- Pollution monitoring
- Anti-poaching surveillance
- Wildfire detection and control
- Crop spraying
- Hobby flying and drone racing
- Video selfies of you or your friends doing cool stuff, like bungee jumping, surfing or white-water rafting
- Surveying or just keeping a general eye on property (if you need an excuse to put a drone on your Christmas list, say that you need it to keep an eye on your roof tiles and gutters)

The hobby-flying market has given us cool names like Parrot Bebop 2 FPV Drone with SkyController 2 and GoPro Karma Drone with Hero6, but generally we still have to choose between longer battery life and higher-resolution imagery. It's only a matter of time before both come together in a single drone at an affordable price and then the sky really will be the limit.

DIGITAL ASSISTANTS

We're talking, of course, about Google Assistant and Amazon Alexa, the main two digital assistants that want to take control of your life in exchange for keeping you company and helping you out in a number of other ways. Other assistants include Siri, Hound and Cortana, but let's take a look at the main features of the Big Two:

	GOOGLE ASSISTANT	AMAZON ALEXA
How to wake them up	'OK, Google'	'Alexa'
Smart speakers	Google Home	Amazon Echo
Artificial intelligence	Hundreds of 'actions', including access to Google Chromecast (for streaming online stuff to your TV), Google Translate (language translation) and quotes from 'Alfred' to suit your mood	Over 25,000 'skills', including access to Amazon Fire, Amazon Prime TV, Amazon Pantry (for home shopping deliveries) and a great link-up to the Sonos One speaker network

Both systems will allow you to remotely control your home, even from the office or the beach, assuming you have installed the correct equipment to make your home 'smart' in the first place. Your voice commands will allow you to operate your smart heating, locks, lights, blinds, curtains, TV recordings and music players. Other everyday tasks and activities they will help you with include physical workouts, recipes, reminders, wake-up calls and weather, news and travel updates.

HACKING YOUR OWN SECURITY

Even if you don't have a smart home, there are some smart things you can do when you're going to be away from your home for any length of time:

Use timer plugs to put lights on and off at the same times they would if you were at home.

Do the same with a radio or smart speaker, because music always makes it sound like there's someone at home.

Have your heating on a timer as a cold house is guaranteed to feel like an empty house (it will also prevent burst pipes in winter).

Have a family member or neighbour pop by to close your curtains at dusk and open them up again in the morning.

Ask whoever delivers your mail to make sure it is left out of sight or, even better, to deliver it to a neighbour. Alternatively, have a family member or neighbour scoop it up.

Forget about all the above by having a family member or someone else in to house-sit while you're away. It costs very little to use trustedhousesitters.com to find sitters who have been vetted by the organisation and you can check out their previous reviews online.

Getting a house-sitter in is even better if you have cats or dogs, because you will save a fortune in cattery or kennel fees.

MAN AND FOOD

Long gone are the days when a man's sole contribution to putting food on the table was to hunt down and kill a woolly mammoth. And even if you sometimes yearn for those simpler times, you know it makes sense in the twenty-first century to understand the need for a balanced diet that contains all the nutrients you need for a healthy, manly lifestyle (in which respect, see also 'Healthy eating' in the Manly Health and Happiness chapter).

In this chapter, we'll have fun with food, looking at famous chefs, man-friendly recipes, BBQ tips, and foodie trivia and hacks, including how to cheat at carbs.

INSPIRATIONAL CHEFS

Some chefs do more than create great dishes because they change the way we think about food or become celebrities beyond their kitchens. Consider the following:

- **Auguste Escoffier (1846–1935):** the chef who gave French haute cuisine to the world while working alongside his friend César Ritz at some of the world's finest hotels, including the Savoy in London. Among the many famous dishes he created were peach Melba and Melba toast, in honour of Australian opera singer Nellie Melba.

- **Caesar Cardini (1896–1956):** the world-famous Caesar salad was knocked up in a hurry in 1924 by the Italian immigrant Cardini in a restaurant in Tijuana, Mexico, when a Fourth of July rush caused by visiting Americans from just across the border had depleted the restaurant's supplies.

- **James Beard (1903–85):** this champion of American cuisine was a cookbook author, teacher and TV personality who mentored generations of professional chefs. Today, the annual James Beard Awards recognise exceptional achievements in the culinary world.

- **Wolfgang Puck (1949–):** the Austrian–American celebrity chef has seemingly won as many awards as he's cooked meals. You know you've made the grade when you get guest appearance slots on *The Simpsons* and *Frasier*.

- **Marco Pierre White (1961–):** has been dubbed 'the first celebrity chef', the '*enfant terrible* of the UK restaurant scene' and the 'godfather of modern cooking'. In 1994, at the age of 33, he was the youngest chef at the time to have been awarded three Michelin stars.

- **Jamie Oliver (1975–):** the chef on a mission to make the world a healthier place eventually shamed the UK government into backing his campaign to introduce schoolchildren to healthier foods.

FOOD TRIVIA

Here are some weird facts to tickle your trivia buds:

- When the first drive-through McDonald's opened in Kuwait in 1994, the queue caused a tailback 11 km (7 miles) long.
- Candied grasshoppers are a popular snack in Japan. So is everything else.
- Knowledge is knowing that a tomato is a fruit. Wisdom is not putting it in a fruit salad.
- Many historians believe the naming of sirloin steak comes from the habit of British monarchs (including Henry VIII) declaring a feast open by knighting the side of beef that had been brought before them with the words: 'Arise, Sir Loin.'
- Tiramisu means 'pick-me-up' in Italian.
- If you've ever wondered what the different names for pasta mean, you could probably work some of them out just by looking at the pasta. If you don't have the pasta to hand, here are some of the main ones translated from Italian into English:

- Spaghetti = thin strings
- Vermicelli = little worms
- Linguine = little tongues
- Cannelloni = large reeds
- Gemelli = twins
- Penne = quill pens
- Conchiglie = shells
- Farfalle = bow ties or butterflies (they're the same word in Italian)
- Fiori = flowers
- Orecchiette = little ears
- Tortellini = little pies

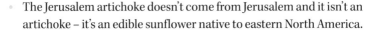

- The Jerusalem artichoke doesn't come from Jerusalem and it isn't an artichoke – it's an edible sunflower native to eastern North America.
- The Swiss consume more chocolate per person than any other nationality, followed by the Germans and then the Irish.
- A lethal dose of chocolate for a human being is about 40 regular bars of milk chocolate.
- The steak dish Tournedos Rossini wasn't just named after the Italian composer; it was likely served up by him after he gave up composing to indulge his other passion of gourmet cooking, having been an excellent amateur chef his whole life.
- Beware hot dogs, which are reported to be responsible for around 20 per cent of deaths by choking each year.
- Fish and chips became a British national dish after Jewish immigrants hit upon the idea of serving chips with their traditional dish of fried fish. They opened the first 'fish and chips' shop in London around 1860.
- The world's most common food allergy is cow's milk, followed by gluten, soya, yeast and egg white. Then comes the peanut, which is the deadliest allergy to have.
- Iceberg lettuce got its name from the crushed ice it was shipped in from California in the 1920s. Until then, it was known as crisphead lettuce.
- Carrots were first grown in Afghanistan, and they were originally purple. The Dutch later modified them to orange in deference to their royal House of Orange.
- If you don't want to cry like a baby while chopping an onion, just stick it in the freezer for 10–15 minutes before you are due to begin chopping.

HOW TO CHEAT AT CARBS

In recent years, we have been given the good news that protein-filled goodies like red meat and eggs are not the arch enemies we were once led to believe they were. In fact, the enemy within has been the evil, sugar-ridden carbohydrate all along, which means that throwing another steak on the barbie has never been healthier!

In other good news, tests in recent years have highlighted a way to reduce 'bad carbs', i.e. the ones that turn into sugar. First, food scientists showed that you could reduce the carbs in bread by around 40 per cent just by freezing and then toasting it, whether you defrost it first or not. It's got something to do with the freezing and defrosting processes making it harder for enzymes to break starch down into sugar.

They carried out their experiments using white bread, which is traditionally considered to be the most evil bread that ever existed, so you can cut down even more by using bread that has fewer carbs to begin with, especially the lesser-known sprouted bread, which is much better for you because it has more fibre and lots of naturally occurring vitamins and proteins.

The same food scientists then did some more tests, which proved that you can reduce the bad carbs in pasta by about 50 per cent if you just cook it, let it cool down and then reheat it before adding your sauce.

So, there you have it: guilt-free bread and pasta. Enjoy.

FOODIE QUOTES

GOOD FOOD IS THE FOUNDATION OF TRUE HAPPINESS.

Auguste Escoffier

• • • • • • • • • •

MY DOCTOR TOLD ME I HAD TO STOP THROWING INTIMATE DINNERS FOR FOUR UNLESS THERE ARE THREE OTHER PEOPLE.

Orson Welles

FOODIE JOKES

WHEN I WAS A BOY, I HAD A DISEASE THAT REQUIRED ME TO EAT DIRT THREE TIMES A DAY. IT'S A GOOD THING MY OLDER BROTHER TOLD ME ABOUT IT.

• • • • • • • • •

TWO CANNIBALS ARE EATING A CLOWN. ONE SAYS TO THE OTHER: 'DOES THIS TASTE FUNNY TO YOU?'

Let's have a look at some recipes we can try ourselves, starting with one that is ideal on a winter's night.

MAN CHILLI

SERVES: 8

Prep: **30 minutes** | Cook: **1 hour 30 minutes**

INGREDIENTS

- 2 kg (4 lb 7 oz) cubed lean beef
- 2 tbsp olive oil
- 3 red chilli peppers, chopped (including seeds)
- 3 large onions, chopped
- 6 cloves garlic, chopped
- 2 tins chopped tomatoes
- 2 tsp hot chilli powder

- 4 tsp ground cumin
- 2 tsp paprika
- 2 tsp sugar
- 1 tsp cayenne pepper
- 1 tsp oregano
- 2 beef stock cubes
- 2 tins red kidney beans
- salt and pepper

COOKING

- Fry the beef in half the oil in a large pan over a high heat until brown.
- Crumble in the stock cubes and stir.
- In a frying pan or wok, fry the chilli peppers, onions and garlic in the remaining oil on a medium heat.
- Add the browned meat and remaining ingredients (except the beans) to the peppers, etc. and simmer for at least an hour.
- Stir from time to time, adding water if and when necessary.
- Add salt and pepper to taste.
- Add the kidney beans 10 minutes before the end.

 COTTAGE PIE

Another great winter warmer.

SERVES: 4

Prep: **10 minutes** | Cook: **1 hour**

INGREDIENTS

- 1 onion, chopped
- 1 clove garlic, chopped
- 2 tbsp olive oil
- 1 beef stock cube
- 1 kg (2 lb 3 oz) minced beef
- 1 tin chopped tomatoes
- 1 tbsp tomato purée
- 1 tsp mixed herbs
- salt and pepper
- 5 medium potatoes (peeled and quartered)
- butter
- milk

COOKING

- Heat the oil in a largish saucepan on a medium heat and add the onion and garlic. Fry for 3 to 4 minutes.
- Add the meat and cook for another 10 minutes until browned.
- Add the stock cube (dissolved in a little water) and other ingredients (except the potatoes) and simmer for 25 minutes.
- While the simmering is going on, boil the potatoes in a separate pan.
- When the potatoes are boiled (a knife should pass through them easily), mash them up with a large knob of butter and a large splash of milk.
- Add salt and pepper to taste.
- Put the meat in a medium-sized ovenproof dish and cover with the mashed potato, then put under the grill until the potato browns slightly.

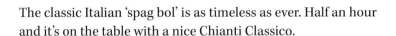

SPAGHETTI BOLOGNESE

The classic Italian 'spag bol' is as timeless as ever. Half an hour and it's on the table with a nice Chianti Classico.

SERVES: 6

Prep: **20 minutes** | Cook: **50 minutes**

INGREDIENTS

- 1 large onion, chopped
- 2 cloves garlic, chopped
- 2 tbsp olive oil
- 1 kg (2 lb 3 oz) minced beef
- 100 g (3½ oz) mushrooms
- 3 rashers bacon
- 1 large carrot

- 1 tin chopped tomatoes
- 1 large glass red wine
- 1 tbsp tomato purée
- 375 ml (13 fl oz) beef stock
- salt and pepper
- 400 g (14 oz) spaghetti
- fresh Parmesan

COOKING

- Fry the onion and garlic gently (it's important not to burn them) in the oil in a large saucepan for 5 minutes.
- Add the minced beef and continue frying for a further 10 minutes.
- While the beef is browning, cut the mushrooms and bacon into small pieces and grate the carrot. Then add these along with the other remaining ingredients.
- While your sauce is reducing, which takes around 20–30 minutes, cook a pasta of your choice – it doesn't have to be spaghetti – according to the instructions on the packet.
- Drain the pasta and put it back into its saucepan.
- Pour the Bolognese sauce on top of the pasta and stir it in well.
- Serve in pasta bowls and grate the fresh Parmesan on top.

✕ CHICKEN IN BEER ✕

I'm beginning to wonder if we don't have a bit of a theme developing here, what with all that alcohol that seems to go so well with manly dishes.

SERVES: 4

Prep: **20 minutes** | Cook: **1 hour 15 minutes**

INGREDIENTS

- 1 onion, chopped
- 2 tbsp olive oil
- 4 large chicken pieces
- 3 carrots
- 1 leek
- 100 g (3½ oz) washed button mushrooms
- 1 large can of your favourite beer
- salt and pepper

COOKING

- Fry the onion in the oil in a flameproof casserole dish on a medium heat for 3 to 4 minutes.
- Add the chicken and fry for another 10 minutes, turning once.
- While the chicken and onion are frying, slice the carrots, leek and mushrooms and chuck them in the dish along with the beer and seasoning, then stick in the oven for 1 hour at gas mark 5/190°C/375°F.
- Help yourself to another beer or two so that the chicken doesn't get to have all the fun.
- Serve with chunks of fresh bread and butter.

✕ VEGETABLE STIR-FRY ✕

If you fancy a bit of a detox day, lay off the booze and have yourself a super-healthy stir-fry.

SERVES: 2
Prep: **15 minutes** | Cook: **10–15 minutes**

INGREDIENTS

- 1 onion, chopped
- 1 clove garlic, chopped
- 1 carrot, chopped
- 1 red pepper, chopped and deseeded
- 1 green pepper, chopped and deseeded
- 250 g (9 oz) spring greens
- 2 tbsp olive oil
- 1 tin bamboo shoots
- 2 tbsp soy sauce
- salt and pepper
- handful of fresh beansprouts

COOKING

- Pour the oil into your wok or frying pan over a high heat.
- As soon as the oil begins to smoke, reduce to medium heat, add the onion and garlic and fry for 4 minutes, stirring constantly.
- Add the spring greens and keep stirring for a couple more minutes.
- Add the soy sauce, seasoning and other vegetables (except for the beansprouts).
- After frying for another 5–8 minutes (depending on how crispy you like your stir-fry), add the beansprouts and cook for no more than another couple of minutes in order to keep the beansprouts firm.

CHICKEN CURRY (INDIAN STYLE)

If you want to try your hand at making your own curry, start with this simple chicken version.

SERVES: 4

Prep: **20 minutes** | Cook: **45 minutes**

INGREDIENTS

- 2 onions, chopped
- 2 cloves garlic, chopped
- 2 tbsp olive oil
- 3 tsp curry powder
- 1 tsp garam masala
- 3 fresh green chilli peppers
- 400 g (14 oz) diced chicken breast
- 2 tbsp water
- 1 tin chopped tomatoes
- 3 whole green cardamom pods
- 2 tbsp fresh coriander, chopped
- 1 small pot natural yoghurt
- salt and pepper
- boil-in-the-bag rice of your choice

COOKING

- Fry the onions and garlic in the oil in a large saucepan on medium heat for 4 minutes, or until they have softened.
- Chop the chillies into rings while you're waiting.
- Add the curry powder, garam masala and chillies and fry for a couple more minutes.
- Add the chicken and water and fry for 5 more minutes.
- Add the chopped tomatoes, cardamom pods and simmer for 25 minutes.
- Season to taste, add the chopped coriander and simmer for 5 more minutes.
- Read the instructions on your bag of rice and ensure you cook it in salted boiling water in good time to be enjoyed with the curry.
- Add the yoghurt and serve with your rice of choice

HUNGARIAN GOULASH

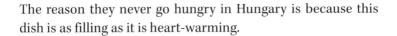

The reason they never go hungry in Hungary is because this dish is as filling as it is heart-warming.

SERVES: 4

Prep: **15 minutes** | Cook: **1 hour 30 minutes**

INGREDIENTS

- 1 large onion, chopped
- 1 clove garlic, chopped
- 2 tbsp olive oil
- 1 kg (2 lb 2 oz) stewing beef, diced
- 1 red pepper, chopped and deseeded
- 1 green pepper, chopped and deseeded
- 1 tin chopped tomatoes
- 1 tbsp smoked paprika
- 1 tsp mixed herbs
- salt and pepper
- 375 ml (13 fl oz) beef stock
- 100 g (3½ oz) mushrooms
- 125 ml (4 fl oz) sour cream

COOKING

- Brown the meat in half the oil over a medium heat in a large saucepan.
- Remove from the pan and set aside.
- Using the same saucepan, fry the onion and garlic in the remaining tablespoonful of oil on a medium heat for 3–4 minutes.
- Add the chopped peppers to the dish along with the browned meat, tomatoes, paprika, herbs, salt and pepper, and cook for about another 5 minutes.
- Add the stock to the pan and simmer on a low heat for about 60 minutes.
- Slice and add the mushrooms.
- Simmer for a further 10 minutes, then add the sour cream.
- Serve with buttered crusty bread.

 PAELLA

Transport your guests to Valencia with this iconic dish.

SERVES: 4

Prep: **25 minutes** | Cook: **1 hour**

INGREDIENTS

- 2 medium onions, chopped
- 2 cloves garlic, chopped
- 1 red or green pepper, chopped and deseeded
- 4 tbsp olive oil
- 200 g (7 oz) round-grain white rice
- 4 medium tomatoes
- pinch saffron
- 500 ml (17 fl oz) chicken stock
- 4 large chicken thighs
- 100 g (3½ oz) frozen peas
- 100 g (3½ oz) cooked mussels (optional)
- 100 g (3½ oz) peeled prawns (optional)
- salt and pepper

COOKING

- Fry the onions and garlic in half the oil in a large frying pan or wok on medium heat for 3–4 minutes. Season during cooking.
- Remove the seeds from the tomatoes (cut in half from side to side – not top to bottom – and squeeze gently until the seeds have all come out).
- Add the rice, saffron, tomatoes and stock, bring to the boil, then cook gently for 10 minutes.
- Fry the chicken on both sides in a separate pan with the remaining oil for 10 minutes or until lightly browned, then add to the rice.
- Stir the chopped pepper and peas into the mix (along with the mussels or prawns if using), and simmer until the rice is cooked (this can take up to another 30 minutes, but keep tasting the rice throughout cooking to check).
- Serve with lemon wedges.

✕ MANBURGERS ✕

Is there anything manlier than a big fat burger, especially when you've prepared and cooked it yourself?

SERVES: 4
Prep: **10 minutes** | Cook: **8–10 minutes**

INGREDIENTS

- 1 onion, finely chopped
- 1 clove garlic, finely chopped
- 1 red chilli (deseeded), finely chopped
- 500 g (1 lb 2 oz) minced beef
- 50 g (1¾ oz) breadcrumbs
- 1 egg
- 1 tsp French mustard
- dash of Worcestershire sauce
- salt and pepper

COOKING

- Mix all the ingredients in a bowl.
- Divide the mixture into four portions, then shape each portion into something that resembles a burger.
- Grill for about 4–5 minutes on each side under a medium grill, or until golden brown.
- Serve in a seeded bun with sliced tomatoes, pickles and a sauce or relish of your choice.
- Wash down with beer.

Tip: if you want to be really manly, don't remove the seeds from the chilli.

 BAKED FISH IN WINE

This is possibly the simplest recipe in the entire world.

SERVES: 2
Prep: **5 minutes** | Cook: **35 minutes**

INGREDIENTS

- 2 cod steaks
- 1 onion, peeled and cut into rings
- salt and pepper
- 1 glass Sauvignon Blanc (or whatever dry white wine you have to hand)

COOKING

- Put the fish in a shallow baking dish.
- Place the onion rings on top of the fish and season to taste (load on that black pepper if that's your thing).
- Pour the wine over the top and bake in the oven for 35 minutes at gas mark 5/190°C/375°F.
- Have a glass or two of the Sauvignon Blanc while you're waiting.
- Served with new potatoes and your favourite steamed vegetables

BEEF AND ALE STEW

Does life get better than beef and beer on the same plate?

SERVES: 4

Prep: **30 minutes** | Cook: **2 hours 15 minutes**

INGREDIENTS

- 3–4 tbsp vegetable oil
- 2 large onions, finely chopped
- 2 medium carrots, peeled and thickly sliced
- 2 celery sticks, trimmed and cut into large pieces
- 400 g (14 oz) tin good-quality plum tomatoes
- salt
- 2 fresh bay leaves
- 2 sprigs thyme
- 1 tbsp flour (seasoned with ½ tsp cayenne pepper)
- 1 kg (2 lb 3 oz) diced braising steak
- 500 ml (17 fl oz) pale ale
- 1 tsp crushed black peppercorns

COOKING

- Heat the oil in a large, heavy-bottomed casserole dish over a medium-high heat. Add the onions, carrots and celery and fry for 4–5 minutes, or until softened but not browned.
- Add the tomatoes, black peppercorns, bay leaves and thyme, and cook, stirring regularly, for a further 3–4 minutes.
- Stir in the seasoned flour and cook for a further 2–3 minutes.
- Add the beef, then pour in the pale ale and bring to the boil. Reduce the heat to low and simmer gently for 2 hours, stirring every 20–30 minutes, until the beef is tender enough to be cut with a spoon.
- Season with the salt. Serve in bowls with thick slices of fresh bread, or on plates with mashed potato and green vegetables.

HOW TO COOK A STEAK

Many men assume grilling is the best way to prepare steak. It isn't. The best way is to fry it in a very hot, heavy cast-iron pan (pans with non-stick coatings get damaged at the high temperature required to cook a steak).

A good steak, whether fillet, T-bone, sirloin, rump or rib-eye, should be allowed to speak for itself, so keep the seasoning simple – salt, pepper and olive oil are the only necessary ingredients. Only pepper should be put on the steak prior to cooking, though. Salt is best added later because it draws out the juices from uncooked meat.

Once your steak is at room temperature (allow one hour out of the fridge), let the pan warm up for a few minutes, then add a teaspoonful of olive oil. As soon as the oil begins to smoke, drop the steak into the pan. It will make an awful noise and it will splatter, so be sure to wear your chef's apron. The steak will immediately stick to the pan, which is fine, so leave it alone. Your cooking times should be as follows:

- Rare: 4 minutes maximum
- Medium: 6 minutes
- Well done: 8 minutes

Turn the steak over in one swift movement every minute or so to ensure an even cook. Salt both sides towards the end.

When the time is up, place the steak on a plate and cover it loosely with foil. Let it sit for 4 minutes to allow its juices to percolate.

Tuck right in or serve in an open crusty bread sandwich if you feel like a bit of a rebel that day.

HOW TO EAT LOBSTER

The lobster shell exists to prevent you from getting to that rich, tender lobster meat. The shell must die.

- Allow the lobster to cool after cooking.
- Remove the large claws from the body by twisting them off at the joints.
- Crack the claws. A nutcracker works well for this.
- Bend the body back from the tail – it will crack, and then you can remove the tail. Break off the small flippers on the tail.
- Push the tail meat out of the tail. It should come out in one piece. If the black vein is still in the tail (ideally, it should have been removed prior to cooking), remove and discard.
- Dip the lobster meat in melted butter and enjoy. Repeat as you kill more and more of the shell.
- Find the liver (it's green) and either eat or discard it. Try not to puke if you eat it.
- Note that the coral-coloured roe in a female lobster is also edible (but only if you're a crazed fool).
- Crack the body apart to find the meat in the four cavities where the legs join the body.
- Also look for meat in the small walking legs if you have a lobster weighing more than 0.9 kg (2 lb). Use a skewer to get the meat out.

HOW TO CARVE A TURKEY

After all those hours of preparation and anticipation (probably on Christmas Day or Thanksgiving, because very few people cook a whole turkey at any other time of the year), be sure to carve the turkey in a way that preserves its flavour and texture.

- Choose a sharp, thin knife with a 10-inch blade.
- Find where the thigh bones meet the body and slip your knife into the joints to separate them.
- Separate the two drumsticks from their thighs by cutting through the joints as you wiggle the drumsticks free.
- Run your knife along the bones to separate the meat from the thighs and drumsticks – try to get as much as possible in one piece.
- Use your knife to separate the wings from each side of the body.
- Carve thin slices off both sides of the breast, cutting parallel to the breast.
- Pause for applause before serving.

DESSERTS

You should always have a couple of go-to, easy-to-prepare desserts in your culinary armoury. Here are two suggestions:

ETON MESS

SERVES: 4
Prep: **10–15 minutes**

INGREDIENTS

- 500 g (1 lb 2 oz) fresh raspberries
- 400 ml (14 fl oz) double cream
- 3 x 7.5 cm (3 in) ready-made meringue nests, crushed
- 1 tbsp ginger cordial
- sprigs of fresh mint

'COOKING'

- Purée half the raspberries in a blender.
- Whip the double cream in a bowl with an electric whisk until stiff peaks form, then add the puréed raspberries and crushed meringue.
- Gently add the raspberries (but reserve a few for decoration) and ginger cordial.
- Spoon equal amounts of the mixture into four cold wine glasses. Serve garnished with the remaining raspberries and a sprig of mint.

 CHEAT'S RHUBARB CRUMBLE

SERVES: 4

Prep: **5 minutes** | Cook: **25 minutes**

INGREDIENTS

- 1 large tin rhubarb in syrup
- packet crumble mix
- 1 tbsp caster sugar

COOKING

- Drain the rhubarb and put it into a pie dish.
- Sprinkle with caster sugar.
- Top with the crumble mix, making sure the rhubarb is completely covered. Put into the oven for about 25 minutes at gas mark 5/190°C/375°F.
- Let it sit for 5 minutes after coming out of the oven. Serve with ice cream or fresh cream.

LICENCE TO GRILL

As soon as the sun comes out, do what man does. Run outside and fire up the barbie. There are about a million books full of recipes if you want to get overly good at cooking stuff on it, but I only have the space here to suggest a few basics to (re)kindle your enthusiasm for the sport. So here are some hints and tips that might just come in handy.

By all means, use a gas grill if you're inexperienced or short of time, but remember that the smoky flavour you get from using charcoal or wood is one of the main ingredients of a barbecue.

You can enhance the flavours yet more by placing some chicory, garlic or herbs on top of the coals or wood.

Don't use lighter fuel instead of crumpled-up newspaper to get your charcoal going. It'll save time, for sure, but it won't exactly enhance the flavour of your food.

Line the bottom of your barbecue with as much aluminium foil as you've got so you can just lift it out and put it straight into the bin the next morning. The lack of mess will cheer you and your hangover right up.

If you use metal skewers, dip them in or wipe them with vegetable oil before skewering your meat and veg. If you use wooden skewers, stop them burning by soaking them in cold water for at least half an hour before using them.

Make your grill non-stick by sticking a fork in the curved side of half an onion and gently rubbing it over your cooking surface. Never cook meat straight from the fridge. Let it come up to room (or garden) temperature to avoid the outside getting charred and the inside not cooking through.

As far as possible, don't cook too many things at once. You'll get confused and your guests will end up having to take pot luck on how well (or not) their food is cooked. Just tell them when it's burger time or corn-on-the-cob time or whatever-else time. They'll be too busy drinking your beer and wine to care when you serve them what anyway.

Cook meat and veg well away from one another on different parts of the grill, especially if you have some vegetarians at your party (they'll explode if they inadvertently eat a piece of meat and nobody wants to see that).

Don't poke your meat while it's cooking. Just leave it alone on a high heat for 3–4 minutes per side, until it goes a bit crusty. Poking it or moving it around on the grill with tongs or spatulas won't make you look as professional as you think. In fact, it'll make you look like a muppet that doesn't understand the need to stop your juices running out the first chance they get.

Use a thermometer if you really need to check how well done your meat is, but only towards the end of the recommended cooking time.

Always let your meat sit for up to ten minutes after you remove it from your grill. This seals in the juices and keeps the meat from drying out. Cut it only when you are ready to serve and eat.

Use a baking tin (the kind that you would use to bake 12 little cakes at a time) to serve up your dips at a barbecue. It looks great, it can't break and it cuts down on washing up afterwards.

TO EGG OR NOT TO EGG, THAT IS THE QUESTION

Eggs used to be good for us (in Britain there was even an Egg Marketing Board to encourage people to eat lots more of them), and then they weren't (because food scientists thought they contributed to high cholesterol levels) and then they were again (because scientists changed their minds). In fact, they are full of useful proteins, minerals and vitamins.

The humble chicken egg is a versatile little thing and we all have favourite ways of cooking and eating them. More exotic varieties from the bottoms of ducks, geese and quails even provide gourmet options. Not wanting to over-egg things here, though, I have chosen a simple, healthy recipe that has the benefit of using up leftovers that you can chuck together quickly and easily at any time of the day, although it's especially good for breakfast the morning after the night before because it's a good 'soaker-upper'.

EGGS WITH ATTITUDE

SERVES: 2

Prep: **5 minutes** | Cook: **10 minutes**

INGREDIENTS

- 2 eggs per person
- a dash of full-cream milk
- a generous grind of black peppercorns (or any pepper that's lying around the kitchen, especially if it's paprika)
- a big pinch of salt (if you use sea, smoked or garlic salt, it'll make you feel like you're a proper cook as well as changing the overall flavour of the dish a bit)
- 2 tbsp grated Parmesan (or Grana Padano)
- 1 tbsp proper butter
- 2 handfuls chopped tomatoes of any colour (even tinned ones will do nicely, but maybe use a teacup instead of your hand)
- 1 handful chopped mushrooms
- anything else you can find and quite like the idea of sticking in there

COOKING

- Preheat a frying pan to a medium temperature.
- Melt the butter (about 30 seconds).
- Add the chopped mushrooms and poke them about a bit for 30 seconds.
- Add the chopped tomato and let it slop around in there for about 3 minutes.
- Break the eggs into a bowl, add the milk, salt and pepper, and fork the mixture around until you consider it to be 'combined'.
- Pour the egg mixture over the contents of the pan, stir it all together very quickly and then turn down the heat to quite low.
- Wait until the eggs look solid and then serve after sprinkling the grated Parmesan on top.
- Serve with strong coffee and lashings of bread and butter.
- Be amazed at how much better it tastes than it looks.

FOODIE QUOTES

THE SECRET OF SUCCESS IN LIFE IS TO EAT WHAT YOU LIKE AND LET THE FOOD FIGHT IT OUT INSIDE.

Mark Twain

• • • • • • • • •

WHAT I SAY IS THAT, IF A MAN REALLY LIKES POTATOES, HE MUST BE A PRETTY DECENT SORT OF FELLOW.

A. A. Milne

FOODIE JOKES

Q. WHY DO THEY ONLY EAT ONE EGG
   FOR BREAKFAST IN FRANCE?

A. BECAUSE IN FRANCE ONE EGG IS AN OEUF.

• • • • • • • • •

I BET MY FRIEND THAT I COULD MAKE A
CAR OUT OF MACARONI. YOU SHOULD HAVE
SEEN HER FACE WHEN I DROVE PASTA.

GREAT FOODIE HACKS

Here are some great 'culinary' tips to make your life a little easier:

Remove the awkward stem from strawberries by pushing a straw all the way through from the bottom. The stem will pop out the top and you can get on with adding black pepper before devouring them.

Turn on the seat warmer in the front passenger seat of your car to keep your pizza (or other takeaway food) warm while you drive home. If you have a passenger, make them sit in the back because the pizza is way more important than they are.

Put your takeaway in the microwave the minute you get home to give yourself time to get out the crockery and cutlery. The microwave is insulated, so you don't even need to turn it on.

Add a teaspoon of baking soda to the water in which you're going to boil your eggs and, once boiled, the shell will come off easily in your hand.

It's better to heat a pizza in the oven, but if you must microwave it, put a small glass of water in beside it to stop the crust going chewy.

HOW HOT IS YOUR CHILLI?

The heat in a chilli pepper is measured by the Scoville scale, invented in 1912 by scientist Wilbur Scoville while working for a pharmaceutical company in America. Here are some examples to show you what it means in practical terms:

CHILLI PEPPER (WITH REGION OF ORIGIN)	SCOVILLE HEAT UNITS (AVERAGE)	WHAT IT MEANS
Bell pepper (Central and South America)	Nil	Might as well suck an ice cube
Padrón (Galicia, Spain)	1,500	Great as a tapa washed down with G&T
Jalapeño (Mexico)	6,000	Not enough to blow your sombrero off
Cayenne (French Guiana)	40,000	Starting to heat up a bit
Habanero (Amazon region, then Cuba)	200,000	Puts you in the mood to dance the salsa
Scotch bonnet (Caribbean)	250,000	Not one to be worn under the kilt
Bhut jolokia or ghost chilli (Indian subcontinent)	1 million	Perfect for curries
Carolina reaper (South Carolina)	1.57 million	Not quite the grim reaper, but heading in that direction
Dragon's breath (UK)	2.48 million	Not one for a first date
Pepper X (South Carolina)	3.18 million	Stand back!

MANLY DRINKS

If you thought hunting down woolly mammoths was a bit passé as a means of getting food on the table, what about beer-swilling? Unless you've had your head stuck in a keg for the past ten years, you must have noticed the beer revolution that has been under way. In this chapter I'll look at what that means, alongside the craft gin and hipster vodka revolutions that are also sweeping the planet. And no, I haven't forgotten about wine, and I'll also explain the difference between whisky and whiskey, and I won't forget about more traditional cocktails either. In fact, this is fast turning into my favourite chapter of the book.

It's even getting easier to drink responsibly these days, as ever-more-sophisticated drinks offer quality rather than quantity, so don't go overdoing it no matter how much fun you're having!

DRINKING TRIVIA

Here are some great facts to get you in the mood for a swift couple of pints or glasses of wine:

- It takes around 700 grapes to make a bottle of wine.
- Russia didn't classify beer as alcohol until 2011, having previously considered it to be a soft drink (which, compared with their vodka, it is).
- Each year, the Czechs drink more beer per person (around 300 pints) than any other nationality in the world, followed by the Namibians (!) and then the Austrians.
- Belgium may be a small country, but it still produces more quality beer than any other nation on earth. At the time of writing, 224 active breweries produce around 800 varieties, most of which are served in their own branded glass. Beers that have been made in Trappist monasteries for hundreds of years are still highly prized.
- As of 2018, the most ever paid for a bottle of wine was US$500,000 for a 1992 Californian Screaming Eagle Cabernet. It was a 6-litre bottle, so a bit more of a bargain than you were probably thinking.
- Vikings drank from the skulls of their defeated enemies, which is the derivation of the Danish–Norwegian–Swedish word 'Skol!', meaning 'Cheers!'
- Absinthe was banned from many countries for a long time because its toxic properties led to alcoholism and mental illness, but a less-toxic version is currently making something of a comeback. Well, they do say that absinthe makes the heart grow fonder.

THE BEER REVOLUTION

You could be forgiven for thinking that craft beer has replaced real ale in recent years, given the marketing hype surrounding the former, but what does it all mean?

Real ale: the term was coined in the UK by CAMRA (Campaign for Real Ale) in the 1970s to distinguish real ale from bland, mass-produced, processed beers. Real ale is fermented in the cask from which it is served, usually via a hand pump, and the carbonation is entirely natural.

Craft beer: served under 'draught/draft' pressure from kegs, not casks. It all started with the Anchor Brewing Company of San Francisco as long ago as 1849 during the California Gold Rush. It is generally served colder than real ale.

Whatever the type of beer, some have been given great names in recent years and are probably worth trying just so you can say 'I tried a Whiplash Bone Machine last night' or 'Would anyone like to try a Fyne Ales Kilkerran Wee Heavy?' Here are some other brilliantly named ones:

- BrewDog Elvis Juice
- Amundsen x Northern Monk Voodoo Headbanger
- Evil Twin Rhubarb Compote Sour
- Yeastie Boys Inari Biru
- Mikkeller I Don't Have a Red Shrimp
- Founders Dirty Bastard
- To Øl Dangerously Close to Stupid Imperial IPA
- Wicked Weed Genesis Blonde Sour
- Buxton x Omnipollo Yellow Belly
- Camden Gentleman's Wit

GUINNESS

World-famous Guinness was first brewed in Dublin way back in 1759. One of the most successful beers ever, it has some pretty impressive stats and facts:

- It is brewed in around 50 countries.
- It is sold in more than 120 countries (out of 195 in the world).
- Around 10 million glasses are drunk around the world each day.
- It got its creamy smooth texture in 1959, when it started to use nitrogen bubbles instead of CO_2.
- Its 'tang' comes from the roasted unmalted barley used in the manufacturing process.
- The harp on Guinness cans, bottles, glasses and other merchandise faces right instead of left to distinguish it from the Irish coat of arms.
- The citizens of the UK and, surprisingly, Nigeria both consume more Guinness than Ireland. Cameroon is another surprise in fourth place, with the USA fifth.
- The company has recently removed isinglass – which comes from the swim bladders of fish – from its fining process so that Guinness can be enjoyed by vegetarians and vegans.
- Guinness may appear black, but it is officially a dark shade of ruby.
- 'Guinness is Good for You' was a popular advertising slogan for Guinness in the 1920s. It probably still is, even if the marketing people aren't allowed to say it any more.

BEER COCKTAILS

If you're tired of old-fashioned cocktails like the Old Fashioned, up your game with the new cocktails in town. Their base ingredient is more flexible than it has been in any time in its history, thanks to a manufacturing revolution and a marketing drive that has it looking sexy, but in a robust, man-about-town kind of way. Yes, we're talking about beer!

ESPRESSO STOUT

A cocktail that doesn't just taste great, it also has a dark, menacing look about it. Better still, it is loaded with caffeine, so don't worry if you're at the end of a long, hard week. A couple of these babies and it's hello Clubsville!

INGREDIENTS

- 30 ml cold espresso coffee
- 30 ml coffee liqueur (e.g. Kahlúa)
- 250 ml stout

MIXING

- Pour the cold espresso into a small jug and add the coffee liqueur.
- Stir and put in the fridge, along with two highball glasses.
- Allow to chill for 30 minutes, then divide the stout between the two glasses and top them up with the espresso mix.

 SPIKED MICHELADA

A cocktail that is every bit as refreshing as it looks and really comes into its own on a hot summer's day.

INGREDIENTS

- 1 whole lime
- 1 lime slice
- 2 tbsp sea salt
- ice cubes
- 1 tbsp tequila
- 330 ml quality lager (e.g. Augustiner Lagerbier Hell)
- Worcestershire sauce

MIXING

- Pour the juice of the whole lime into a small bowl and brush it around the rim of your glass, preferably a tankard.
- Tip the sea salt on to a plate and dip the rim of your glass into the salt to coat it.
- Fill the glass with ice cubes and add the tequila and the remaining lime juice from the bowl.
- Stir gently, then pour in the lager.
- Top with the Worcestershire sauce and slice of lime.

DRINKING QUOTES

TODAY'S RAIN IS TOMORROW'S WHISKY.

Old Scottish proverb

• • • • • • • • • •

THE ONLY CURE FOR A REAL HANGOVER IS DEATH.

Robert Benchley

DRINKING JOKES

THE PAST, THE PRESENT AND THE FUTURE WALKED INTO A BAR. IT WAS TENSE.

· · · · · · · · ·

I WAS SO DRUNK ON ST PATRICK'S DAY I HAD TO TAKE A BUS HOME. THAT MIGHT NOT SOUND LIKE A BIG DEAL TO YOU, BUT I'D NEVER DRIVEN A BUS BEFORE.

WHISKY AND WHISKEY

Here are some facts to Scotch any rumours you might have heard about the world's most famous drink:

Scotch whisky is only allowed to be produced in Scotland, where there are more than 120 distilleries.

The best whisky is generally regarded to be single malt Scotch whisky, which means it is made with malted barley at a single distillery.

The word whisky derives from the Gaelic for 'water of life'.

The Irish translated their original Gaelic word into whiskey with an 'e'. They then took the 'e' with them when they emigrated in huge numbers to the USA, which also, therefore, has an 'e' in its whiskey, as in 'bourbon whiskey'.

Canada and Australia remain true to the original spelling of whisky (presumably because they had many more UK than Irish immigrants over the years), as do the Japanese.

Scotch whisky is made primarily from malted barley; Irish whiskey is made from malted barley often mixed with other grains, e.g. maize, wheat or rye.

Bourbon whiskey is made primarily from corn, whereas Canadian whisky is made from corn with added rye, which they generally drink with ginger ale as a Rye and Dry.

Whisky and whiskey do not mature in the bottle, so a 12-year-old bottle will still be a 12-year-old bottle in 100 years' time. Might as well drink it then.

Whisky distilleries are getting in on the craft gin revolution because they can get a fairly immediate return on their investment. By way of example, the Bruichladdich distillery on the Scottish island of Islay produces The Botanist, a gin that sets itself apart by using botanicals only found on the island.

WHISKY COCKTAILS

Whisky and whiskey also contribute to some great cocktails. But don't go skimping – the better the whisk(e)y, the better the cocktail.

- **Manhattan:** bourbon or rye, sweet vermouth, aromatic bitters and a cherry.
- **The Churchill:** Scotch whisky, sweet vermouth, Cointreau and lime juice.
- **Whisky (or Whiskey) Sour:** Scotch whisky or bourbon or rye, lemon juice, caster sugar, orange peel and a cherry.
- **Irish Coffee:** freshly roasted coffee, Irish whiskey, brown sugar and lightly whipped cream.
- **Rusty Nail:** Scotch whisky and Drambuie liqueur.
- **The Four Horsemen:** Jack Daniel's Tennessee whiskey, Jim Beam bourbon, Johnnie Walker Scotch and Jameson Irish whiskey.
- **Whisky Mac:** Scotch whisky and ginger wine.

And now for two great cocktail recipes to perfect for yourself and your guests at home:

 OLD FASHIONED

The cocktail for a good old-fashioned man's man (think Ernest Hemingway), especially if you're hard enough to have it for breakfast.

INGREDIENTS

- 50 ml bourbon or rye whiskey
- ½ tsp caster sugar
- 2–4 dashes Angostura bitters
- dash of sparkling water
- ice cubes

MIXING

- Spoon the sugar into the bottom of an Old Fashioned glass (obviously).
- Add the bitters and the splash of water.
- Rotate the glass at an angle to 'muddle' the sugar and bitters (you 'muddle' ingredients when you press or rotate them against the side of a glass to release and meld their flavours).
- Add a couple of cubes of ice and pour in the whiskey of your choice.

Tip: if you want to go 'the whole Hemingway', add an equal measure of brandy alongside the whiskey and add a splash of absinthe to the bitters.

 SCOTCH ROYALE

This Prohibition-era cocktail is possibly the simplest one you'll ever make. A 1:1 ratio of Scotch and champagne creates a lovely crisp taste, while extra champagne will sweeten it somewhat.

INGREDIENTS

- single or double measure of Scotch whisky
- champagne (to taste)
- 1 sugar cube
- 1 dash Angostura bitters

MIXING

- Place the sugar cube in a champagne flute.
- Pour in a measure of whisky and add champagne to taste.
- Add the Angostura bitters and stir briefly.

THE GIN REVOLUTION

For the past several years so many new gins have come on the market that it's difficult to keep up. They set themselves apart from one another by using different botanicals, of course, but also by implementing some of the best marketing ever seen in the history of marketing. Here are some of the coolest-looking, coolest-sounding gins to hit the shelves:

Aviation American Gin: owned by Hollywood star Ryan Reynolds and used on Virgin Atlantic in its cocktails. It's a 'New Western' gin, which means it doesn't use juniper as its primary botanical (it uses lavender instead).

That Boutique-y Gin Company Moonshot Gin: you're not going to believe this, but they only use botanicals that have been sent to space in a balloon and exposed to extremely low pressures at 24 km (15 miles) above the earth's surface.

Pinkster Agreeably British Gin: raspberries are the ingredient that gives this gin its pink hue. Get in touch with your smooth side and perhaps even wear a cravat when serving.

Xolato Chocolate Gin: yes, it does taste like chocolate, so if gin and chocolate are your favourite things, you're about to go to heaven.

Monkey 47 Schwarzwald Dry Gin: does what it says on the bottle. It's from the Black Forest region in Germany, it's 47% ABV and there are 47 different botanicals in there. It's so complex that you could spend a whole evening trying to guess what's in it, but after two or three you probably won't give a monkey's.

Sharish Blue Magic Gin: this deliciously smooth, deep-blue Portuguese gin comes in the coolest-looking, low-slung, feet-wide-apart bottle. As if that's not enough, the deep-blue gin itself turns dusky pink when you add tonic.

Navy Strength Cannonball Edinburgh Gin: it doesn't just fire off a broadside on account of its strength (57.2% ABV, which is 100% proof), its flavour also packs a wallop – its botanicals include oriental spices and Szechuan peppercorns.

Uncle Val's Restorative Gin: its retro label suggests it's a cure-all for whatever ails you, and it probably is. It's crispy when it enters your mouth but silky by the time it slips down your throat. I assume that's it healing you already.

GIN COCKTAILS

Gin, of course, is also a fresh, clean base for lots of cocktails, including the following old favourites (followed by two recipes to try mixing at home):

- **Tom Collins:** dry gin, fresh lemon juice, caster sugar, sparkling water, orange peel and a cherry.
- **Gin Fizz:** gin, double cream, egg whites, lemon juice, lime juice, refined sugar, orange flower water and sparkling water.
- **Pink Gin:** gin, bitters and a twist of lemon peel.
- **Riviera Snob:** Aperol, gin, lemon juice, sugar syrup, soda water and a twist of orange peel.
- **Monkey Gland:** gin, freshly squeezed orange juice, grenadine, sugar syrup, absinthe and a twist of orange peel.
- **London Fog:** gin, Pernod and a twist of orange peel.

 FRENCH 75

Invented around a century ago, the kick delivered by this otherwise sophisticated cocktail was said to feel like being shelled by the 75-mm howitzer field gun used by the French in World War One.

INGREDIENTS

- 1 measure of gin
- 15 ml lemon juice
- twist of lemon peel
- 7.5 ml sugar syrup
- champagne
- ice cubes

MIXING

- Pour the gin, lemon juice and sugar syrup into a cocktail shaker containing ice cubes and shake well.
- Strain into a champagne flute.
- Fill to the top with champagne.
- Garnish with the twist of lemon peel.
- Celebrate whatever special occasion you considered worthy of the classic French 75 in the first place.

 THE ELVIS

The bitter notes from the grapefruit juice and ale balance the floral sweetness of the gin and elderflower liqueur. It will all make sense when you try it.

INGREDIENTS

- 50 ml London dry gin
- 100 ml fresh pink grapefruit juice
- 10 ml elderflower liqueur
- India Pale Ale
- twist of grapefruit peel
- ice cubes

MIXING

- Combine the grapefruit juice, gin and elderflower liqueur in a cocktail shaker.
- Fill the shaker with ice and shake until the outside of the shaker is frosty (about 30 seconds).
- Strain into a tumbler filled with ice.
- Top off with ale.
- Garnish with the twist of grapefruit peel.

THE VODKA REVOLUTION

Not wanting to be outdone by the gin revolution, craft vodka (often dubbed 'hipster vodka' in the media) is also now making a huge splash of its own around the world. Here are just some of the very different vodkas you might like to ask for if you have a birthday coming up:

Reyka Vodka: made with Arctic spring water and distilled near Reykjavik in Iceland. Clean enough to drink on its own.

Debowa Polska Military Vodka: Polish vodka with hints of spice and elderberry. Presented in the shape of a bullet with an oak casing and a copper head, which makes it a great-looking present.

Fair Quinoa Vodka: as smooth as you would expect from a drink that emanates from Cognac in France and the quinoa leaves you with a nice, nutty aftertaste. It's the world first fair-trade vodka because the Bolivian farmers who grow the quinoa are guaranteed a fair wage.

Skyy Premium American Vodka: uses the finest Midwestern grains to produce a clean finish which is perfect as a cocktail base.

Ogilvy Scottish Potato Vodka: smoothly warm in the mouth with a finish of black pepper and charcoal. Great in any weather, but especially nice in front of a log fire in the middle of winter.

Firestarter Vodka: produced in Moldova since the nineteenth century using its finest wheat and brought bang up to date with a bottle that looks like a fire extinguisher, which makes it another great gift.

Black Cow Pure Milk Vodka: made entirely from cow's milk in England, it has a creamy texture but it still tastes like fresh, crisp vodka.

Burnett's Maple Syrup Vodka: one of many flavoured vodkas to burst on to the market. Others include popcorn, salmon, chilli and salted caramel marshmallow.

VODKA COCKTAILS

And let's not forget that vodka is another wonderfully clean base for all manner of cocktails, including the following classics plus two recipes with a twist to try out for yourself:

- **Screwdriver:** large ice cubes, vodka, freshly squeezed orange juice, Angostura bitters, wedge of orange.
- **Bloody Mary:** ice cubes, vodka, tomato juice, Worcestershire sauce, Tabasco, coarse sea salt, black pepper, fennel seeds.
- **Moscow Mule:** crushed ice, vodka, ginger beer, ginger bitters, slice of lime and sprig of mint.
- **Black Russian:** lots of ice cubes, vodka, Kahlúa or Tia Maria.
- **Vodka Martini:** vodka, dry vermouth, Angostura bitters, sugar (to coat the rim of the glass).
- **Sex on the Beach:** ice cubes, vodka, orange juice, peach schnapps, cranberry juice, crème de cassis, swimming costume, deck chair.

 VODKA AND ORANGE

Well, vodka **in** an orange, actually. Perfect for a picnic if you don't want to cart a heavy bottle and glasses around with you:

INGREDIENTS

- large oranges
- premium vodka miniatures (one for each orange)

MIXING

- Take one large orange at a time and use your multitool (e.g. Swiss Army knife) to gouge out a hole the size of a miniature vodka bottle neck.
- Remove one miniature vodka bottle top.
- Place the hole you have gouged in the orange over the neck of the upright opened miniature vodka bottle.
- Turn the orange upside down while holding the miniature vodka bottle with your other hand.
- Wait until all the vodka has flowed inside the orange and then remove the miniature vodka bottle.
- Repeat until you have one vodka in an orange for everybody at the picnic.
- Wait 10 minutes and then have everyone drink the vodka from the hole in the orange.

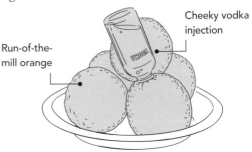

Run-of-the-mill orange

Cheeky vodka injection

THE VICAR'S BLOODY MARY MIX

A simpler version of the acclaimed cocktail that is touted as the perfect Sunday morning hangover cure. You've got nothing to lose anyway.

INGREDIENTS

- ice cubes
- 50 ml vodka
- 100 ml tomato juice
- 50 ml orange juice
- Worcestershire sauce

MIXING

- Put three or four cubes of ice in a glass as quietly as you possibly can.
- Pour in the vodka, tomato juice and orange juice.
- Add as much Worcestershire sauce as you can stomach.
- Take a deep breath.
- Knock it back.
- You're good to go.

→ SPIRITED NON-ALCOHOLIC ← COCKTAILS

The world has finally been blessed with its first alcohol-free spirit. It's called Seedlip and it's a natural, healthy substitute for gin or vodka if you're a soft drinker or designated driver, or if you just fancy a night off the booze. No longer do you have to feel awkward standing at a party like a teenager with a Coke or glass of lemonade in your hand.

It comes in three different combinations of botanicals, herbs, fruits and spices – Garden 108, Grove 42 and Spice 94 – and there is a cocktail book that contains 100 non-alcoholic recipes using one or the other of those three offerings. Cheers!

PRE-DINNER COCKTAILS

Craft gin and hipster vodka might be getting all the headlines these days, but we shouldn't forget that there are other spirits and cocktails out there as well, including some old favourites to loosen the tongue in time for a bit of gossip round the dinner table (plus two more recipes to try at home, including one that will require you to get your toolkit out!):

Singapore Sling: gin, cherry brandy, grenadine, Benedictine, orange juice, lime juice, Angostura bitters, an orange slice and a cherry.

Daiquiri: white rum, caster sugar and a wedge of lime.

Margarita: tequila, triple sec, lime juice, flaked salt and a wedge of lime.

Sidecar: cognac, triple sec, lemon juice and orange peel.

Long Island Ice Tea: vodka, gin, white rum, tequila, triple sec, fresh lemon juice, honey syrup, cola and a twist of lemon peel.

Tequila Sunrise: tequila, lime juice, crème de cassis, sparkling water and a slice of orange.

Dirty Martini: gin, dry vermouth, olive brine, a green olive and a twist of lemon peel.

 NEGRONI

No cocktail has enjoyed such a revival in recent times as the humble Negroni, just in time for the 100th anniversary of its invention in 1919 by the eponymous Italian, Count Negroni:

INGREDIENTS

- 25 ml gin
- 25 ml Campari
- 25 ml sweet vermouth
- 6–8 cm strip of orange peel
- large ice cubes

MIXING

- Fill an Old Fashioned glass halfway to the top with ice cubes.
- Pour in the spirits in any order you like.
- Stir well.
- Heat the orange peel and drape it over the rim of the glass, but with most of the peel inside the drink to give it a bit of zest.

Tip: do as the Italians do on a special occasion and ask your bartender to add prosecco into the mix to create a Negroni Sbagliato (*sbagliato* is the Italian word for 'wrong' or 'mistaken', but they mean it in a good way here)

 FRESH PIÑA COLADA

The best cocktail to make by far, because you get to use a hammer, a chisel, a screwdriver and a cleaver! You'll also need a decent blender. Make sure you follow the safety advice and never make them after you've been drinking them yourself!

INGREDIENTS

- whole coconut
- whole pineapple
- bottle of Bacardi rum
- ice cubes

MIXING

- Having clamped the coconut in a vice, use a hammer and clean screwdriver to poke a hole in at least two of the eyes of the coconut.
- Remove the coconut and drain its water through the holes into your juicer.
- Wrap the coconut in a tea towel and tap with the hammer until you hear cracking. Still using your hammer, split the coconut into as few pieces as possible.
- Clamping the pieces of coconut into the vice one by one, carefully chisel each chunk of white flesh away from its husk using the hammer and chisel, then chuck the chunks into the blender.
- Remove both ends of the pineapple with a clean cleaver and stand it flat on one end.
- Carefully cleave the skin off the pineapple (use the chisel – as opposed to your fingers – to hold the pineapple down while you operate the cleaver with your other hand).
- Cut up the pineapple and throw the pieces into the blender with the coconut. Blend away.
- Fill some glasses up with ice cubes and pour 50 ml Bacardi and 100 ml of the coconut and pineapple mix into each glass.
- Serve wearing your toolbelt (but not just your toolbelt).

WINE

Choosing the right wine for the right occasion can be a bit of a nightmare, unless you're a trained sommelier or a bit of a wine buff. There are about 50 million books and websites, or so it seems, to guide you through the process of buying wine to go with canapés, starters, main courses and desserts, but by far the most sensible thing to do if you're a bit flummoxed is to go to a reputable wine merchant. Tell them your specific requirements and act upon their advice. If you buy your wine at the supermarket, be sure to read what it says on the label as there is often food-pairing information on there to guide you.

If you're dining in a fairly posh restaurant on a special occasion and you're happy to pay a bit more than usual, your waiter will of course be happy to advise you. Otherwise, stick to the house wine – the restaurant has chosen it for most of its customers to drink and they will want you to enjoy it and come back again.

To give you a rough idea, though, here are some basic pairing suggestions to think about the next time you go shopping or dining out:

WINE (RED)	EXAMPLE FOODS
Pinot Noir	Roast vegetables, pâté, lean meat, crème brûlée
Zinfandel	Spicy or barbecued meat, dark desserts
Syrah	Lamb, pasta with tomato sauce, stuffed mushrooms, chocolate mousse
Cabernet Sauvignon	Duck, lamb, beef, stinky cheese, bittersweet chocolate
Merlot	Mature cheese, salmon, tuna, veal, dark berry desserts
WINE (WHITE)	**EXAMPLE FOODS**
Sauvignon Blanc	Oysters, goat's cheese, lobster, shrimp, chicken, sorbet, lemon meringue pie
Riesling	Calamari, creamy cheese, pork, chicken, baked apples
Chardonnay	Seafood, cream-based sauces, hummus, mild cheese, cheesecake
Pinot Grigio	Antipasti, risotto, lobster, white sauces, apple tart

VINO DE NARANJA (ORANGE WINE)

The alternative of orange wine is trending all over good wine bars and restaurants. It's not made from oranges; it just has an orange hue because its white grapes are fermented in their skins. Its deep flavour is rich in tannins, which is why it will happily cut through olives, charcuterie, smelly cheese and dessert. It will even stand in for red wines with a roast dinner.

HACK TO SAFELY
STACK YOUR BEERS

If you're fed up with your beer rolling all over the fridge, just attach a large bulldog clip to one of the bars on one of the shelves. This will prop up your bottom row of beers, which will then act as the base for a whole pyramid of beers that won't be rolling anywhere. If you have glass shelves, just bookend the bottom row with something solid like an old plastic milk bottle full of water.

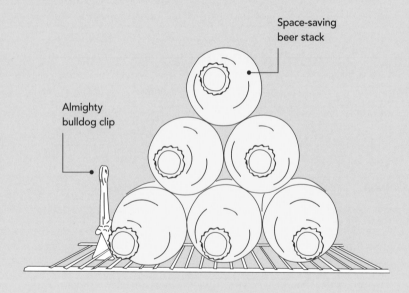

Space-saving
beer stack

Almighty
bulldog clip

DRINKING QUOTES

IN WINE THERE IS WISDOM, IN BEER THERE IS STRENGTH, IN WATER THERE IS BACTERIA.

David Auerbach

* * * * * * * * * *

ALCOHOL IS NECESSARY FOR A MAN SO THAT HE CAN HAVE A GOOD OPINION OF HIMSELF, UNDISTURBED BY THE FACTS.

Finley Peter Dunne

DRINKING JOKES

A THREE-LEGGED DOG WITH A STETSON ON ITS HEAD AND A SIX-SHOOTER ON ITS HIP WALKS INTO A BAR AND SAYS: 'I'M LOOKING FOR THE MAN WHO SHOT MY PAW.'

• • • • • • • • •

ME: CAN I GET A GLASS OF WINE, PLEASE?

EMPLOYEE: SIR, THIS IS A McDONALD'S.

ME: OH, I'M SORRY, CAN I GET A McWINE, PLEASE?

GREAT DRINKING TIPS

Here are some great tips to help you get tipsy:

If you forget to chill your beer, wrap each bottle in a wet paper towel and put it in the freezer for 15 minutes, by which time they will be verging on ice cold.

Put frozen grapes in glasses of white wine to keep them cool without watering down the wine.

If you can't find a corkscrew to open your bottle of wine, improvise with a screwdriver, a claw hammer and a one-inch screw. Screw the nail halfway into the cork and then use the claw of the hammer to prise the cork out on the screw.

If you have wine left over at the bottom of a bottle, freeze it in an ice-cube tray to use later for cooking or as ice cubes to keep your wine cool without watering it down (just make sure it's the same wine you use them in).

HOW TO COPE WITH A HANGOVER

There is no real physical cure for a hangover (other than death, of course) but here are some of the things that might at least lift your spirits on a hangover day:

- A hot shower
- A massive fried breakfast
- Strong coffee
- The hair of the dog (see The Vicar's Bloody Mary Mix cocktail recipe in 'The vodka revolution' section)
- Coconut water: it's purported to have electrolytes that the body craves following overindulgence
- Food packed with vitamins, like oranges, which will also refresh you a bit

In actual fact, the best thing you can do is drink as much water as you can and put your feet up in front of the TV for a good binge watch. It's what Netflix was made for. Just be grateful you're not Mongolian – the only cure you would be offered is pickled sheep's eyes in tomato juice. I, for one, would be doing a sharp ewe turn if faced with that.

Tip: you can take preventative action these days by drinking organic wines, which are free from the pesticides, allergens and sulphites used to grow and ferment just about everything else. You are much less likely to get a hangover if you don't consume these problematic ingredients in the first place. More and more bio wines are now appearing on supermarket and wine merchant shelves, and the quality is getting better all the time.

SPORTING CHAPS

Whether you're a regular participant or spectator, or both, this chapter has something for you. From the Grand Slams of tennis to the Super Bowl of American football, from the four Majors of golf to the Tour de France cycling race, we will cover the globe as we look at the world's sports, homing in on the most popular ones and celebrating the inspirational sportsmen who excel in their individual or team sports. And we will, of course, remind ourselves of the awe-inspiring feats of the Summer and Winter Olympic Games every time they come around. Let's start, though, with some sporting activities that only the roughest and toughest need apply for.

IF YOU THINK YOU'RE HARD ENOUGH

Some sports need a bit more than just skill and determination. Here are some of the ones that only supermen are drawn to, because they involve a high risk of injury to life and limb, or at the very least your dignity:

Ski flying: like Olympic ski jumping, but with faster speeds off longer hills. The time you spend in the air and the distances you can reach are up to 66 per cent greater than those achieved in ski jumping. If you get it wrong, it's probably going to hurt up to 66 per cent more as well.

High diving: the highest board for competitive diving is 10 m (33 ft) and at least you get to land in water with this sport, but belly-flopping hurts if you get it wrong, as does accidentally hitting the board on the way back down from your initial somersault into the air. Progress to World Series cliff diving if you want to freefall from up to 27 m (88 ft) while performing acrobatics.

Heavyweight boxing: boxing at any weight must hurt a bit, but imagine being pounded by more than 90 kg (200 lb) round after round. The American fighter Joe Louis is widely regarded to be the best heavyweight ever, having remained undefeated as world champion between 1937 and 1949.

Kickboxing: if boxing doesn't do it for you, try kickboxing, where you can kick and punch your way to victory. Aim for the Glory World Series, where the minimum weight is 95 kg (209 lb).

Sumo wrestling: if you're prepared to enter a communal training stable, do and eat what you're told for years on end and then grapple in a ring with another huge wrestler wearing a very limited amount of cloth, this is the sport for you.

Caber tossing: if you can throw into the air a bit of tree that is 5.94 m (19 ft 6 in) long and weighs 79 kg (175 lb) and land it on its other end, you may proudly refer to yourself as a 'tosser'. If you don't get the technique right, you may proudly refer to yourself as a 'tosser with a bad back'. Either way, be careful not to get your kilt caught up in the proceedings.

Steeplechasing: jumping over fences on a powerful horse inevitably results in you falling off and breaking bones. The Northern Irish rider Tony McCoy was a champion jockey for a record 20 consecutive years despite breaking bones in every part of his body over that same period. Injuries can and do happen to the horses as well.

Rodeo: you need physical strength and no small amount of nerve to want to ride a stressed bull or bucking bronco, and you can double that for jumping off your horse to wrestle a steer to the ground with your bare hands.

SPORTING TRIVIA

Sport can be a very serious business these days, but it has always managed to throw up some surprising and often amusing facts:

The national game of Afghanistan is polo, except the ball is a headless goat carcass. The Afghans have been introducing more rules in recent times in the hope of getting goat-grabbing accepted as an Olympic sport.

In ancient Mayan ball games, some or all of the losing team were decapitated in a ritual sacrifice to the gods. 'Shall we make it the best of three games?' were the commonest final words uttered by members of the losing team.

In 1974, some villagers on the Pacific island nation of Vanuatu were asked to 'land dive' (the precursor of bungee jumping but using vines from the forest instead of elastic ropes) for the entertainment of the visiting British Queen. Being the wet season, the vines were not all sufficiently elastic to break the fall of the contestants and Her Majesty watched on in horror as one villager plummeted to his death.

The oldest continuous competition in sport is the America's Cup, held every three or four years between two ocean-going sailing yachts. The New York Yacht Club won every trophy for 132 years until the Royal Perth Yacht Club of Australia finally ended its winning sequence in 1983.

The boxer Mike Tyson's debts at the time of his bankruptcy in 2003 included £264,000 for an unpaid birthday party and £5,000 in care for his pet tigers.

Kite flying is a professional sport in Thailand.

The world's ten most popular sports at the time of writing, according to Internet views, are as follows:

SPORT	VIEWS
Football (soccer)	3.5 billion
Cricket	2.5 billion
Field hockey	2 billion
Tennis	1 billion
Volleyball	900 million
Table tennis	850 million
Baseball	500 million
Golf	450 million
Basketball	400 million
American football	400 million

GIANT STADIUMS

At the time of writing, the world's largest stadium by capacity is in North Korea and the next eight are all American football stadiums. Here are the top 12 worldwide:

RANK	STADIUM	CAPACITY	LOCATION	PRIMARY SPORT
1	Rungrado 1st of May Stadium	150,000	Pyongyang	Soccer and gymnastics
2	Michigan Stadium	107,601	Ann Arbor, Michigan	American football
3	Beaver Stadium	107,572	State College, Pennsylvania	American football
4	Ohio Stadium	104,944	Columbus, Ohio	American football
5	Kyle Field	102,512	College Station, Texas	American football
6	Neyland Stadium	102,455	Knoxville, Tennessee	American football
7	Tiger Stadium	102,321	Baton Rouge, Louisiana	American football
8	Bryant–Denny Stadium	101,821	Tuscaloosa, Alabama	American football
9	Darrell K. Royal Texas Memorial Stadium	100,119	Austin, Texas	American football
10	Melbourne Cricket Ground	100,024	Melbourne	Cricket
11	Camp Nou	99,786	Barcelona	Soccer
12	Estadio Azteca	95,500	Mexico City	Soccer

SPORTY QUOTES

I ALWAYS TURN TO THE SPORTS PAGES FIRST, WHICH RECORD PEOPLE'S ACCOMPLISHMENTS. THE FRONT PAGE HAS NOTHING BUT MAN'S FAILURES.

Earl Warren

• • • • • • • • •

IF GOD INVENTED MARATHONS TO KEEP PEOPLE FROM DOING ANYTHING MORE STUPID, THE TRIATHLON MUST HAVE TAKEN HIM COMPLETELY BY SURPRISE.

P. Z. Pearce

SPORTY JOKES

IT'S A GOOD IDEA TO BEGIN AT THE
BOTTOM IN EVERYTHING, EXCEPT
WHEN LEARNING TO SWIM.

• • • • • • • • •

ALL THINGS ARE POSSIBLE, EXCEPT FOR
SKIING THROUGH A REVOLVING DOOR.

• • • • • • • • •

FOUR OUT OF FIVE DENTISTS
RECOMMEND PLAYING ICE HOCKEY.

OLYMPIC GAMES

There's no bigger sporting event than the Olympic Games, and there is no shortage of amazing facts and figures to remind us why:

SUMMER OLYMPICS

Following the 2016 Rio Games, the USA had amassed 2,520 Summer Olympic medals since the modern games began in 1896, followed by Russia (1,865) and Germany (1,681).

At the time of writing, American swimmer Michael Phelps, aka the 'Flying Fish', is the most successful Olympian of all time, with 28 medals, including 23 gold (which is more than 66 countries have achieved in total).

The American black athlete Jesse Owens won four gold medals (100 m, 200 m, long jump and 4 x 100 m relay) at the 1936 Berlin Olympics to spoil Adolf Hitler's public statements about Aryan supremacy (although Owens wasn't invited to the White House to be congratulated by Franklin D. Roosevelt either).

In the 1928 Amsterdam Olympics, Australian rower Henry Pearce stopped to let a family of ducks cross his lane and still won the gold medal.

The youngest winner of an Olympic medal was Dimitrios Loundras, a ten-year-old Greek gymnast who won bronze at the 1896 Athens Olympics.

Painting, sculpture, architecture, literature and music were Olympic events from 1912 to 1948. Jack Yeats, the brother of poet W. B. Yeats, took the painting silver medal at Paris in 1924 to win Ireland's first ever Olympic medal.

Other ex-Olympic events include the following worthy (and one not-so-worthy) sports:

- standing high jump
- tug of war
- two-handed javelin
- tandem cycling
- underwater swimming
- equestrian long jump
- croquet
- one-handed weightlifting
- solo synchronised swimming (as recently as 1992)
- obstacle swimming race (which involved scrambling over and under rows of boats)
- duelling pistols (using human silhouettes dressed in frock coats as the targets)
- live pigeon shooting (nearly 400 birds were killed within a small area and the resulting scene was one of carnage)

WINTER OLYMPICS

The Winter Olympics are literally way cooler than the Summer Olympics and Norway is the coolest competing country by a long way, with 329 medals and counting, including the record-breaking 12 won by their cross-country skier Bjørn Dæhlie.

Downhill skiers reach speeds of up to 145 kph (90 mph).

The first figure-skating gold medal was won at the London 1908 Summer Olympics (16 years before the first Winter Olympics at Chamonix) by Ulrich Salchow, whose backwards take-off jump is still used today.

The Jamaican bobsleigh team made history in Calgary in 1988 when they became the first team from a tropical country to compete in a Winter Olympics. They crashed out, but not before other teams had lent them their spare sleds and given them whatever coaching they could. The 1993 movie *Cool Runnings* is based on their story.

Another famous underdog at the same games was English ski jumper Eddie 'The Eagle' Edwards. He came last in both the 70 m and 90 m events and had his story immortalised in the 2016 movie *Eddie the Eagle*.

PARALYMPICS

The Paralympics are the second-largest multisports competition in the world after the Olympic Games, with more than 4,000 athletes representing 160 countries (compared with around 11,000 athletes representing around 190 countries at the Olympics).

The Greek word *para* means 'beside', hence the Paralympics are the 'parallel games'.

The Canadian swimmer Michael Edgson is the most successful male Paralympian to date, having won 18 gold medals across three games.

The South African double amputee Oscar Pistorius was a popular athlete known as 'the Blade Runner'. He won six Paralympic medals and would probably have won more had he not been convicted of killing his girlfriend in 2013.

The Spanish Paralympic basketball team that won gold at the Sydney games in 2000 later had to hand their medals back, after ten of them were found not to have a disability.

For many, the most popular Paralympic event is 'murderball', the name originally given to the wheelchair rugby event in which upended wheelchairs are considered to be a perfectly normal part of the game.

FOOTBALL (SOCCER)

Football (or soccer, if you prefer) has become a billion-pound industry across the globe, with players and managers earning ludicrous sums of money and referees struggling to control the antics of prima donna players. Supporters of the game remain fiercely loyal to their teams and favourite players, though, however painful that might be at times. Here are some of the reasons why:

The Brazilian player Pelé was football's first superstar celebrity, after starring for his country in the 1958 World Cup at the age of just 17.

Today, the debate continues to rage over who has been the world's best player in recent years: the Portuguese player Cristiano Ronaldo (450 goals and 119 assists in 438 appearances for Real Madrid between 2010 and 2018) or the Argentinian Lionel Messi (472 goals and 176 assists in 476 appearances for Barcelona over the same period).

To date, Brazil has won the World Cup a record five times, followed by Germany and Italy (four wins each) and Argentina, France and Uruguay (two wins each).

The UEFA Champions League in Europe is the most prestigious club competition in the world. Here is a list of the most successful teams in the competition (up to and including 2018):

- Real Madrid (13)
- AC Milan (7)
- Bayern Munich (5)
- Barcelona (5)
- Liverpool (5)
- Ajax Amsterdam (4)
- Internazionale (aka Inter Milan) (3)
- Manchester United (3)

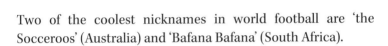

Two of the coolest nicknames in world football are 'the Socceroos' (Australia) and 'Bafana Bafana' (South Africa).

In the 48 hours following England's loss to Argentina in a World Cup penalty shoot-out in 1998, the number of heart attacks in England went up by 25 per cent.

In 2002, in protest against refereeing decisions that had gone against them in earlier matches, a league team in Madagascar lost 149–0 to their main rivals by scoring 149 own goals without letting their opponents touch the ball.

The San Marino international football team has only ever won one match (out of 154 at the time of writing), which was a 1–0 victory in a friendly against Liechtenstein in 2004. It does hold the record for scoring the fastest World Cup goal in history, though, after just 8.3 seconds in a World Cup qualifier against England.

At the Eidi Stadium in the remote Faroe Islands, the players sometimes have to lie down flat until the wind abates enough for them to continue. If the wind carries a ball out to sea, there are fishermen waiting in rowing boats on the choppy ocean to retrieve it.

RUGBY

Rugby union took off when young William Webb Ellis supposedly picked up the ball and ran with it during a football (soccer) match at Rugby School in England in 1823. Here are some facts to convert you if you're not already a diehard fan:

The USA were the reigning Olympic rugby champions from 1924 until 2016, but only because rugby wasn't an Olympic sport between those years. It was reintroduced at the Rio Olympics as rugby sevens.

Since the Rugby Union World Cup was inaugurated in 1987, it has been dominated by teams from the southern hemisphere (three wins for New Zealand and two each for Australia and South Africa), with England the sole winners from the northern hemisphere.

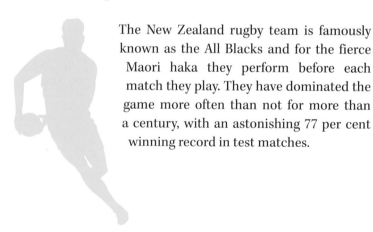

The New Zealand rugby team is famously known as the All Blacks and for the fierce Maori haka they perform before each match they play. They have dominated the game more often than not for more than a century, with an astonishing 77 per cent winning record in test matches.

The most exciting end to a Rugby Union World Cup final came in 2003 when England's Jonny Wilkinson scored a drop goal right at the end of extra time to snatch victory from host nation Australia.

Rugby league, which broke away from rugby union in 1895, is played at a faster pace with fewer players (13-a-side as opposed to 15-a-side) and quicker restarts after play has broken down. Of the 15 Rugby League World Cups held since inauguration of the competition in 1954, Australia have dominated with 11 wins, the other four being won by Britain (3) and New Zealand (1).

CYCLING

Competitive cycling takes many forms, but road racing is the one that gets the most attention. Cycling has also become a mass-participation activity around the world. Here are some facts to get you fired up to join the current revolution:

As if the five one-day classics, known as 'the Monuments', weren't tough enough, cycling also offers its hardest competitors three annual stage races, known as the Grand Tours, with each lasting for three weeks:

- Giro d'Italia
- Tour de France
- Vuelta a España

The greatest road-racer ever is the Belgian Eddy Merckx, who won a record 11 Grand Tours (five Tours de France, five Giri d'Italia and one Vuelta a España) and all five Monuments (Milan–San Remo, Tour of Flanders, Paris–Roubaix, Liège–Bastogne–Liège and Giro di Lombardia). He was nicknamed 'the Cannibal' in view of his insatiable appetite for eating up miles.

British cyclist Bradley Wiggins is the only cyclist to ever win an Olympic gold medal and the Tour de France in the same year.

The most successful bike racer in Tour de France history was the American Lance Armstrong, until it was finally established in 2012 that he had taken performance-enhancing drugs throughout his career. His seven wins were subsequently removed from the records.

In the second ever Tour de France in 1904, many of the competitors were disqualified for jumping on trains or taking lifts in cars during the night.

The Dutch use their bicycles for one in three of all journeys made, compared with one in a hundred in the USA.

The number of bicycles and cars in the world are both over a billion, but twice as many new bicycles as cars are now being made each year.

GOLF

The game that started on windswept sandy dunes in Scotland centuries ago is now a global phenomenon that thrills us every year with four major championships: the US Masters, the Open Championship (which is always played on a seaside links course around the British coastline), the US Open Championship and the US PGA. Here are some great golfing facts to get you into the swing of things:

To date, the most successful men's golfer of all time is the American Jack Nicklaus, with 18 major championships – four more at the time of writing than fellow American Tiger Woods.

Tiger Woods' real name is Eldrick Tont Woods.

The first Ryder Cup was played between the USA and Britain in 1927. Ireland joined in with Britain in 1953, as did the rest of Europe in 1979. Overall, the USA has won 26 of the 41 matches that have been contested. In the 20 matches to date since the format became Europe v USA, Europe has won 11 and the USA has won eight, with one match tied.

At the time of writing, the Englishman Nick Faldo has scored more Ryder Cup points than anyone else with a total of 25 points over 11 consecutive appearances.

Golf is popular in North Korea, ever since Kim Jong-il played his one and only game of golf in 1994 and scored a remarkable 38-under-par round of 34 that included 11 holes-in-one. That was according to his official biography, so there is no reason to doubt it.

Japanese golfers take out insurance against the risk of getting a hole-in-one, because tradition dictates that they should celebrate the unlikely event by throwing a party complete with significant gifts for all of their friends.

To date, there are more than 15,000 golf courses in the USA alone, which is almost half the number of courses in the entire world. Appropriately enough for the home of golf, though, Scotland has more golf courses per capita than any other country, followed by Ireland, New Zealand and Australia.

When American astronaut Alan Shepard played two six-iron shots on the moon in 1971, one ball went into orbit and the other ended up in a crater, making it the only hole-in-one recorded on the lunar surface to date.

CRICKET

This quintessential English summer game spread around the British Empire in the seventeenth century to become one of the most played and watched sports worldwide. Here are some facts to bowl you over:

The Australian cricketer Don Bradman is the greatest batsman to have ever played the game, with an average of almost 100 runs in all Test matches. Sachin Tendulkar (India) isn't far behind, having scored a hundred centuries himself. Other great batsmen have been Brian Lara, Viv Richards and Clive Lloyd (all West Indies).

Muttiah Muralitharan (Sri Lanka) is generally considered to be the best bowler of all time, having taken 800 wickets in Test matches with his off-spin deliveries. He took his 800th and final Test wicket with his last delivery in his last Test match in 2010. The leg-spinner Shane Warne (Australia) is the only other bowler to have exceeded 700 Test match wickets (708).

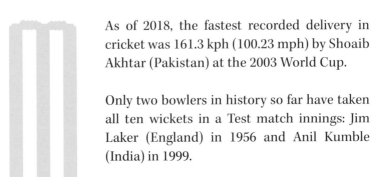

As of 2018, the fastest recorded delivery in cricket was 161.3 kph (100.23 mph) by Shoaib Akhtar (Pakistan) at the 2003 World Cup.

Only two bowlers in history so far have taken all ten wickets in a Test match innings: Jim Laker (England) in 1956 and Anil Kumble (India) in 1999.

Great all-rounders who were equally proficient with bat and ball have included Gary Sobers (West Indies), Ian Botham (England), Kapil Dev (India) and Imran Khan (Pakistan).

Imran Khan, who scored 3,807 runs and took 362 wickets in Test matches, later became the prime minister of Pakistan.

At the time of writing, Graham Gooch (England) holds the record for most runs scored in a Test match (across two innings), with 456 runs against India in 1990.

To date, Brian Lara holds the highest ever individual innings score in a Test match, with 400 not out against England on Antigua in 2004.

One Day International (ODI) cricket was added in 1971 to bring cricket up to date in a fast-moving world and led to the first ODI World Cup in 1975. Of the 11 competitions to date, Australia have won five and India and the West Indies have each won two (Pakistan and Sri Lanka are the other winners).

Only three batsmen have scored a double century in an ODI game to date, and they are all Indian (Sachin Tendulkar, Virender Sehwag and Rohit Sharma).

TENNIS

One of the most popular sports played and watched worldwide, the tempo can be fierce and skill levels are often off the scale. Here are some facts to get you reaching for your racket:

A player's place in history is largely determined by how many Grand Slams (Australian Open, French Open, Wimbledon and US Open) they win. Here is how things stood in men's tennis at the end of 2018:

- Roger Federer (Switzerland): 20
- Rafael Nadal (Spain): 17
- Pete Sampras (USA): 14
- Novak Djokovic (Serbia): 14
- Roy Emerson (Australia): 12
- Rod Laver (Australia): 11
- Björn Borg (Sweden): 11

The longest match in tennis history was at Wimbledon in 2010, when the American John Isner finally beat French player Nicolas Mahut 6–4, 3–6, 6–7, 7–6, 70–68 after 11 hours and 5 minutes over three days.

The Croatian player Goran Ivanišević is the only Grand Slam champion with a name that alternates consonants and vowels. He is also credited with serving the most aces in a single year, in 1996, when he notched up 1,477.

The fastest serve ever recorded in tennis was in 2012, when the Australian player Sam Groth hit the ball in at 263.4 kph (163.7 mph).

RUNNING

The simplest sport of all, because all you need is yourself and a pair of running shoes to get started, but some go on to take it very seriously indeed:

Roger Bannister (1929–2018): the Englishman made history in 1954 when he broke the four-minute barrier for the mile. The record is now 3:43:13, set by Moroccan runner Hicham El Guerrouj in 1999.

Michael Johnson (1967–): the Texan was the most consistent sprinter in athletics history, never losing a single Olympic or World Championship final. He won four Olympic gold medals and eight World Championship gold medals in 12 races between 1992 and 1997.

Mo Farah (1983–): the British runner from Somalia achieved the 'quadruple double' by winning the 5,000 m and 10,000 m at consecutive Olympics and consecutive World Championships.

Eliud Kipchoge (1984–): the Kenyan runner won the Olympic marathon at the Rio 2016 Olympic Games and is the current marathon world-record holder with a time of 2 hours 1 minute 39 seconds. At the time of writing, he has won 11 of the 12 marathons he has entered, including three consecutive London and Berlin Marathons.

Usain Bolt (1986–): the Jamaican runner is widely considered to be the best sprinter of all time, having won double gold in the 100 m and 200 m at three consecutive games (Beijing, London and Rio).

A HACK THAT WILL SAVE YOUR SKIN

There are certain sports that are literally more irritating than others, especially running and cycling. Anything that involves extended periods of regular movement at anything above walking speed causes friction at the contact points, which means your nipples, inner thighs and groin are going to get well and truly chafed if you don't protect them.

Petroleum jelly is the answer, so get smearing before it's too late.

A dab will do!

Do not use in place of petrol or jelly

PETROLEUM JELLY

FORMULA 1 MOTOR RACING

If you feel the need for speed, here are some facts to keep you in the fast lane:

The German racing driver Michael Schumacher won a record seven F1 championships between 1994 and 2004. Juan Manuel Fangio (Argentina) won five in the 1950s and British driver Lewis Hamilton drew level with him when he won for the fifth time in 2018.

Formula 1 drivers have to withstand 5G of force (five times their own bodyweight) under braking and cornering and can lose up to 5 kg in a single race.

Scuderia Ferrari have won the Constructors' Championship 16 times, with Williams (9) and McLaren (8) trailing behind. Mercedes are the form team, though, having won five consecutive championships between 2014 and 2018.

Formula 1 cars are built to the limits of the latest technology, with each team guarding their own latest developments under great secrecy. Here are some of the amazing facts we do know about the cars:

- The cost of the 800,000 or so components in each car is around US$7 million.
- Because they rotate 50 times per second at top speed, the tyres only last for 90–120 km (55–75 miles).
- The indestructible carbon fibre of the brake discs will withstand the heat of molten lava.
- The engines can last for just two hours of racing before blowing up.
- The cars race at speeds of up to 360 kph (224 mph) and can take just four seconds to accelerate to 160 kph (100 mph) and return to 0.

AMERICAN FOOTBALL

The National Football League (NFL) consists of 32 teams, 16 each from the National Football Conference (NFC) and the American Football Conference (AFC). Starting in 1967, the season culminates each year in the Super Bowl, when the two Conference winners compete for the coveted Lombardi Trophy. Here are some great NFL and Super Bowl facts:

As of 2018, the Pittsburgh Steelers have won the most Super Bowls (six). The New England Patriots, Dallas Cowboys and San Francisco 49ers all have five.

Roman numerals are used to depict the consecutive numbering of Super Bowls. For example, the 53rd Super Bowl played in early 2019 is designated Super Bowl LIII.

Pre-game and half-time musical acts have become a much-anticipated event within the Super Bowl spectacle. Famous performers to have enjoyed the privilege include The Who, Bruce Springsteen, Madonna, Lady Gaga, Beyoncé, Lenny Kravitz, Prince, The Rolling Stones, U2, Britney Spears, Stevie Wonder, Smokey Robinson, James Brown, Michael Jackson, Paul McCartney, Chubby Checker and Ella Fitzgerald.

American football has become so popular in the UK that NFL league games have been played to large crowds at London's Wembley Stadium since 2007.

The Dallas Cowboys are the most valuable sports team in the world, having been valued by Forbes at US$4.2 billion in 2018, just ahead of the Manchester United, Real Madrid and Barcelona soccer clubs.

Tom Brady, the quarterback for the New England Patriots, is the most successful player in Super Bowl history so far, with a record eight appearances, winning five and being awarded MVP (Most Valued Player) at four.

Over Super Bowl weekend, Americans will consume well over a billion chicken wings, 8 million pounds of guacamole and 50 million cases of beer.

The average playing time in an American football game of four quarters (i.e. one hour) is about 12 minutes, but you have to allow about three hours to include breaks for hot dogs.

It takes around 600 cows to make the footballs required for each NFL season.

Cheerleading causes more serious injuries to women in the USA than any other sport.

OTHER MAJOR NORTH AMERICAN SPORTS

The Super Bowl isn't the only show in town when it comes to sport in North America. Here are some of the other major ones:

Baseball: the MLB (Major League Baseball) season finishes each year with the World Series, a best-of-seven play-off between the winners of the American League and the National League. The Toronto Blue Jays are currently the only Canadian team to participate.

The most famous baseball player of all time was Babe Ruth, who smashed all previous home-run records while playing for the New York Yankees in the 1920s. The Yankees are also way ahead of all other teams at the time of writing, with 27 World Series wins since the inception of the competition in 1903.

Basketball: the NBA (National Basketball Association) is the top professional basketball league in the world. It has 30 teams, including the Toronto Raptors, the sole Canadian representative. The most successful team in NBA history so far is the Boston Celtics, with 17 titles. They are closely followed by their arch rivals, the Los Angeles Lakers, who have won 16 titles. In more recent years, though, the Golden State Warriors of the San Francisco Bay Area have been the form team.

Six-times NBA Champion (and MVP on each occasion), Michael Jordan is arguably the best player ever, although others might argue for the equally famous Magic Johnson or the 2.16 m (7 ft 1 in) Shaquille O'Neal.

Hockey: the NHL (National Hockey League) has 31 teams, 24 from the USA and seven from Canada. The Stanley Cup is awarded to the champions at the end of each season and as of 2018 has been won the most times (23) by the Montreal Canadiens, followed by the Toronto Maple Leafs (13). The most famous player in NHL history is Canadian Wayne Gretzky, with more goals and assists than any other player. At the time of writing he still holds 61 NHL records in spite of having retired from the ice in 1999.

Soccer: the sport has grown exponentially in the USA and Canada in recent times. The MLS (Major League Soccer) has 23 teams, 20 in the USA and three in Canada. The league winners are awarded the Supporters' Shield and a further play-off competition leads to the MLS Cup, which was inaugurated in 1996. LA Galaxy are the most successful team, with five wins, and their superstar players have included Zlatan Ibrahimović, Steven Gerrard and David Beckham. D. C. United, who themselves signed English superstar Wayne Rooney in 2018, are currently running second with four MLS Cup wins.

Other major Canadian sports: Canada has hockey, baseball and basketball in common with the USA, but lacrosse, wrestling and curling are also hugely popular, and soccer has become the country's most popular sport of all in terms of participation.

AMERICAN SPORTING TRIVIA

Never say you're a big football fan if you mean soccer, and don't go to a hockey match expecting to see sport on terra firma (as opposed to body smashes on ice). Here are some great sporting facts from across the pond:

- The basketball court on the fifth floor of the Supreme Court building in Washington, D. C. is known as 'the highest court in the land'.

- In 2000, Pope John Paul II was made an honorary Harlem Globetrotters basketball player when the team visited him at the Vatican, although ice hockey and skiing were the Pope's sports of choice while growing up in Poland.

- After American basketball player Michael Jordan signed up with Nike in 1984, he made more money in sponsorship from the company in a year than all the Nike factory workers in Malaysia combined.

- Baseball may be the USA's national sport, but it is also the most popular sport in Japan. At international level, Japan is regularly ranked number one ahead of the USA.

- Legendary (ice) hockey injuries have included the following:
  - A goalie set on fire when the puck struck a box of matches he had in his pocket.
  - A player's jugular vein being split open by an errant stick (the player survived after his trainer reached into his neck and pinched off the bleeding until medics arrived).
  - A spectator being beaten with his own shoe after a player took exception to something he shouted out.
  - A bat that was fatally mistaken for the puck when it flew across the ice.

SPORTY QUOTES

THE TOUR DE FRANCE PRODUCES IN ME SUCH PERSISTENT SATISFACTION THAT MY SALIVA FLOWS IN IMPERCEPTIBLE BUT STUBBORN STREAMS.

Salvador Dalí

• • • • • • • • • •

BASEBALL IS 90 PER CENT MENTAL. THE OTHER HALF IS PHYSICAL.

Yogi Berra

SPORTY JOKES

BEFORE YOU CRITICISE SOMEONE, YOU SHOULD RUN A MILE IN THEIR SHOES. THAT WAY, YOU'RE A MILE AWAY AND YOU HAVE THEIR SHOES.

· · · · · · · · · ·

GOLF AND SEX ARE THE ONLY THINGS YOU CAN ENJOY WITHOUT BEING GOOD AT THEM.

· · · · · · · · · ·

IF YOU WANT TO KNOW WHAT YOU'LL LOOK LIKE IN TEN YEARS' TIME, LOOK IN THE MIRROR AFTER YOU'VE RUN A MARATHON.

MAN STYLE

Men have been caring about their appearance since the dawn of time. Some trends come and go, and quite often come back again. Others never go away. Fashions over the past century have included top hats and flat caps; two-toned gangster shoes and loafers; baggy, bell-bottomed and flared trousers; flower-power shirts and graphic T-shirts; cravats, neckties and polo necks; and, of course, ubiquitous denim jeans and trainers. There have been so many styles, in fact, that vintage and retro male clothing is now a huge industry in itself.

Hairstyles also come and go, from the crewcut to the man bun. Facial hair ranges from designer stubble to the 'full set' (full beard and moustache). There are so many grooming products out there for men today that it's difficult to know which oil, putty or gel to buy for which part of the anatomy.

This chapter looks at how we should dress to impress and the importance of self-grooming to the modern man.

INSPIRING MEN OF FASHION

Before we get started on how we should dress and groom ourselves, let's take some inspiration from some great style icons past and present:

James Dean: the blueprint for casual cool. Jeans, black leather jacket, white T-shirt, sunglasses. Sorted.

David Bowie: the chameleon singer changed his style more times than most of us have been clothes shopping. His looks included 1960s Mod, space-age flamboyance, gentlemen's club, experimental, camp, glam rock and hippie.

Ralph Lauren: never less than elegant himself, he launched his menswear Polo look on the world in 1968 and went on to add women's clothing, fragrances for both sexes and a homeware range across the globe.

Gianni Versace: the Italian designer brought vivid colours and bold prints into mainstream fashion. Traditional fashion designers disapproved of his 'bad taste' but the people who mattered, the ones with money to spend, soon proved him right and them wrong.

Paul Smith: although mostly known as a clothes designer, the creative genius has also turned his hand to the design of homeware, motorbikes, book covers, bicycles, cycling wear, the Evian water bottle, a camera, a set of postage stamps, a Bowie album cover, a range of wine bottles, the Anglepoise lamp, a range of luxury pens and a Porsche 911. He's one cool guy.

Pharrell Williams: forever pushing fashion to the limits with his unique styles, the award-winning rapper, singer, writer and producer owns streetwear brands Billionaire Boys Club and Ice Cream.

David Gandy: the supermodel who brought muscle to a fashion industry that had only previously employed men who went missing when they turned sideways. He soon became the face (and body) of Dolce & Gabbana and went on to write for *Vogue* magazine, create his own clothing range and race powerboats and cars, including in the classic Mille Miglia car endurance race.

David Beckham: not content with being one of the greatest soccer players to ever play the game, Becks has been a style icon since he got his first pay cheque from Manchester United. Effortlessly impeccable is the look he achieves whether wearing a tailored suit or a T-shirt and jeans. He has experimented with hairstyles, which have been mostly successful, and has committed to more than 40 tattoos.

Matt Smith: arguably the coolest Doctor to ever appear on the BBC's iconic *Doctor Who* programme. His ability to throw anything together and look great on the red carpet whatever he's wearing prompted *GQ* magazine to name him their Best Dressed Man 2018.

Skepta: the grime and rap artist has been setting trends for more than ten years now and his latest designer-meets-streetwear look has a massive following both on and off the music scenes he commands.

THE ESSENTIAL WARDROBE

What's cool and what isn't is very much a matter of individual opinion when it comes to clothing, but there are some things that we should all be aware of if we want to look smart enough to impress, land a job, get dates or just feel good about ourselves when we walk out of the front door. Let's take a look at some essentials.

Suit: your options include plain, stripe, check or herringbone as your basic pattern; cotton, wool, linen, tweed or velvet as your cloth; a two-piece or three-piece combination; and a single-breasted or double-breasted jacket. Whatever your choice, it really does pay to have at least one good suit made to measure. It will fit you like a glove and you will be able to have a say in the finer details, including lapels, pockets, vents and buttons.

Casual jacket: get yourself a bomber jacket or a utilitarian denim jacket that you can wear over anything at a moment's notice. Smarten them up in seconds with a soft scarf tied round the neck and hanging down the chest.

Shirts: dress shirts with collar and cuffs are versatile enough to be worn with or without a tie, and with a smart suit or a pair of jeans. The important thing is that they should fit well. Polo shirts and T-shirts are ideal as casual wear. Mix and match to your heart's content, though – wearing a plain T-shirt under a very smart suit, for example, is one of the greatest smart-casual looks known to man.

Ties: although becoming less fashionable by the minute in the more relaxed culture of the twenty-first century, there are occasions when you will need one, such as a job interview with a non-tech company or a smart wedding. Try to keep them plain if you need them to be versatile, but you could go for knitted ones if you want to look modern as well as smart.

Trousers and jeans: if you're reading this on the other side of the pond in the USA, I'm talking pants here. If you're reading this north of Hadrian's Wall, I'm talking about breeks or trews. Wherever you are, you don't need me to tell you that denim jeans are the most versatile form of clothing known to man, but do also keep some smart-casual chinos in your wardrobe for occasions like meeting your future parents-in-law for the first time.

Accessories: in the liberal twenty-first century, you can go way beyond watches, rings and cufflinks. Think man bags and jewellery and build up a selection of hats for different outfits. Even make-up for men is making a comeback (it was perfectly acceptable in Ancient Egypt and was still mainstream in eighteenth-century France), with specialist parlours and heaps of online advice about what's right for you, depending on whether you want to go subtle or bold.

NO PANTS DAY

The idea of riding the subway wearing no pants (trousers) started in New York in 2002 and has since spread to cities around the world. It happens in early January, causing Berliners on one occasion to participate in sub-zero temperatures. Fortunately or unfortunately, depending on your point of view, the London version sticks to the American meaning of pants.

SHOES

There is an old saying that 'shoes maketh the man' and I always notice if someone in my company is wearing well-made, well-looked-after shoes, even if I'm slopping about in trainers myself at the time. Here are some of the great shoes you should have in your wardrobe if you can afford them:

Classic Oxford: simple, stylish and elegant. Also durable on account of their Goodyear welted construction. Buy a black and a brown pair because one or the other will go with most suits you ever buy.

Brogue: similar to the Oxford, but with lots of holes punched in them by way of decoration. Especially useful for weekends on Highland country estates, because they even look good with formal wear and kilts.

Spectator: the two-tone classic popularised by American gangsters and often copied by golf-shoe manufacturers.

Chelsea boot: all the rage in the swinging sixties, this staple comes in a variety of smart and casual styles They have an elastic side panel and a loop at the back to make it easy to get them on and off.

Comfortable: for everyday life away from the workplace, and particularly when going on holiday, you need some sneakers, trainers, deck shoes or whatever you feel comfortable in for the climate and terrain you're going to find yourself in. Maybe try Skechers 'lifestyle' shoes, which are as light as air but provide good support while looking a bit smarter than trainers.

STYLE TIPS FOR YOUR FEET

GO FOR QUALITY

Buy as many good-quality shoes as you can afford, because the less you wear each pair, the longer they'll last. Also look after them well, which takes time, effort and proper shoe polish – follow the instructions on the tin, which will include great advice like leaving the polish on for a few minutes before starting to buff it off again.

GO SOCKLESS IF YOU WANT

One fashion that is bound to divide men is wearing shoes with cropped trousers and no socks, which has seen something of a revival in recent times. It certainly looks great on Daryl, my unfeasibly cool, young nephew, but dissenters rant about the sweat, smell and infection that the sockless must surely suffer. You'll be fine, though, if you just look after the inside of your shoes and wear low-cut loafer socks or cedar insoles that nobody can see. Some designers are even producing shoes that are comfortable and hygienic enough inside not to need socks in the first place.

Just don't make the mistake that many men made the last time the sockless look was in fashion, which was to liberally apply talcum powder to their feet and the inside of their shoes. It turned up everywhere they put their hands for the rest of the day, which sometimes must have proved a bit embarrassing.

DRESS FOR YOUR BODY SHAPE

It's possible to book a personal shopper to advise on your current wardrobe and on which styles and colours you should choose when shopping – it all depends on your height, shape and skin tone.

For example, there are different rules for a vertically challenged man and a tall man, or if you're a bit on the thin side, or if you've been eating too many pies. Our natural torso shape (rhomboid, triangle, inverted triangle, rectangle or oval) also dictates what we should wear, and there are lots of websites to advise you on that (e.g. www.theidleman.com). Here are just a few points to illustrate the sort of things you need to be considering:

MEDIUM TO TALL MEN

Should avoid tight-fitting clothes that will pinch in all the wrong places when they move their long limbs around.

Double-breasted jackets and waistcoats are good 'fillers' for the tall, slim man.

Eye-catching belts are useful to break up the height.

Lighter shades present less of a solid mass.

Short sleeves or short shorts have a tendency to make tall men look like an overgrown schoolboy.

If you're tall and carrying a bit of excess baggage, make sure you buy generous sizes so that you don't look as if you're trying to burst out of your clothes.

SHORT TO MEDIUM MEN

Should wear clothes that are fitted, not baggy.

Shorter jackets work best, especially casual jackets fitted at the waist.

Heels and hats add height.

Wearing different colours on the top and bottom, especially with a belt in between, cuts a short person in two and accentuates the shortness of both halves.

Wearing the same tone from top to bottom, on the other hand, has the effect of lengthening the body.

Long shorts below the knee will make you look like an oompa loompa.

These rules are especially important if you're carrying a bit of a paunch.

Whatever shape, size or height you are, however, the most important thing is to wear the right clothes with confidence. Posture is crucial and standing up straight exudes confidence.

COLOUR CO-ORDINATION

In order to find out which colours suit your skin tone and eye and hair colours, you can check out any number of online resources or even attend a class for the day. There are also some dos and don'ts, whatever your personal colours are:

- Once you understand your personal colour chart, put whole outfits together with colours that are side by side on your chart. Using layers (e.g. a matching T-shirt under a smart shirt or hanging below your jumper) will add texture and interest.
- Black shoes are a sensible option with black, blue or grey trousers (but not with jeans).
- Wear brown shoes with any colour of trousers.
- Ties are best kept plain if you want to tone them in with your entire outfit.
- If you're more about having a bit of fun than being regarded by your peers as a classy dresser, go for loud, patterned ties and socks that scream 'LOOK AT ME, I'M MORE IMPORTANT THAN THE REST OF THE OUTFIT'. There are certainly plenty to choose from nowadays, especially around Christmas.

STYLISH QUOTES

YOU CAN NEVER BE OVERDRESSED OR OVEREDUCATED.

Oscar Wilde

• • • • • • • • •

CLOTHES MAKE THE MAN. NAKED PEOPLE HAVE LITTLE OR NO INFLUENCE ON SOCIETY.

Mark Twain

STYLISH JOKES

MEN WHO SHAVE SPEND ROUGHLY 3,350 HOURS OF THEIR LIFE IN THE BATHROOM. MEN WITH BEARDS USE THAT TIME TO HAVE FUN WITH THE PARTNERS OF MEN WHO SHAVE.

* * * * * * * * * *

I USED TO BE ADDICTED TO SOAP, BUT NOW I'M CLEAN.

* * * * * * * * * *

WHEN AN AMERICAN MOTHER TOLD HER YOUNG SON THAT HE HAD TO WEAR A LONG-SLEEVED SHIRT TO GO TO HIS BIG SISTER'S WEDDING, HE PLEADED THE SECOND AMENDMENT. WHEN HIS MOTHER ASKED HIM WHAT HE WAS TALKING ABOUT, HE SAID: 'I HAVE THE RIGHT TO BARE ARMS.'

UNDERSTANDING HAIRSTYLES

Take a good, long look at yourself in the mirror. Decide whether your hair is straight, wavy, curly or thinning, and whether the shape of your face is oval, square, round or diamond. Then read the following tips:

Straight hair: a short, classic hairstyle is in order because long hair is going to just hang there looking sorry for itself. Unless you want a ponytail, in which case go for it.

Wavy hair: unless you're a bit OCD, don't worry about trying to control or straighten your hair. Just let it grow long enough to show the waves you've been given.

Curly hair: your hair has so much texture you can do what you want with it, including a mop of curls or even dreadlocks.

Thinning hair: play your hair at its own game and thin it right down to the same height with some head trimmers. Facial hair looks great with a shaved head, so see the 'What to do with your face' section in the pages that follow.

Oval face: short back and sides is good, but you need a good bit of hair on top to avoid rounding your face into the shape of a football. Long hair also works.

Round face: you were born a soccer ball, so you need to oval your face a bit with some thickness up top. If you're happy to sculpt it up a bit, even better. Never have a fringe, because it'll just tempt people into kicking your head.

Square face: you can round your top corners by shaving your head, or you can draw attention away from your angles with a fringe or anything else that allows some hair to cover your forehead.

Diamond face: stop people staring at your pointy jawline with any hairstyle that adds interest. Anything slightly off-piste will do, even if it's just running some putty through it in the morning. Alternatively, just add facial hair – but not a pointy beard, obviously.

HAIR PRODUCTS

If you need some help to achieve the right look for the head you've been given, the following are available online and in every supermarket and pharmacy/drugstore in the free world:

Wax: gives good hold and structure to straight or wavy hair, and you can choose between matte and shine finishes. Just rub it through from root to tip with your fingers.

Paste and clay: good hold with low shine. Useful for thinning hair as the matte finish adds substance.

Gel and mousse: it's OK for a quick fix, but it's really the poor relation of wax and clay.

Putty and fibre: strong hold with no shine. Use putty for short hair and fibre for longer or thicker hair. Pay attention while you're applying them because you won't be able to comb your hair afterwards.

Cream: use to slick hair back and achieve the Brylcreem look of British fighter pilots during World War Two. Ronald Reagan kept the look alive even after the Beatles popularised dry hair.

Pomade: a step up from cream if you have thicker hair or if you want your hair to stay in place forever. Pomade was first made popular when it was used to create the pompadour hairstyle in eighteenth-century France and back then it was made with bear fat or lard. By the time it roared back into popularity on account of Don Draper's hairstyle in the AMC TV series *Mad Men*, it was made of lanolin, petroleum jelly or beeswax.

Relaxer: if you have naturally curly hair and don't want it, perhaps because it's just too difficult to manage, you can straighten it with a hair relaxer (a type of lotion or cream designed for the purpose).

Hairspray: whichever of the above products you use on your hair, and even more so if you use none of them, hairspray is perfect for locking your hair in place. Today it comes with cool names like Fudge Unleaded Skyscraper Spray.

Hair tonic: currently enjoying a revival as a styling aid after being ousted for a while by inferior gel and mousse. They mostly come in liquid form, which makes them great for a scalp massage, but they also come as a spray, including the magnificently named Lock Stock and Barrel Prep Tonic Thickening Spray.

Hairbrush or comb: use a wide-toothed comb for curly hair, a soft brush for fine hair and a stiff brush for everything else.

GROOMING HACKS

USE THE RIGHT SHAMPOO FOR YOUR HAIR:

- For shorter, finer hair, look for the ingredients of keratin and amino acids to add some volume.

- For longer, thicker or curlier hair, look for moisturising shampoos to relax your mop.

- For oily hair, look for a rebalancing formula and only shampoo every other day.

HOW TO AGE GRACEFULLY:

- Wear your distinguishing grey hair with confidence (think George Clooney) or keep it short and use a grey-hair shampoo to tone it down.

- If you feel the need to dye your hair, make sure the colour matches the tone of your skin. By way of example, jet-black hair with a pale complexion is bound to frighten small children. Seek advice from your hair stylist if needs be. If you don't want to be found out on a first date, make sure you dye elsewhere while you're about it.

- If your hair has started to thin out, attack it with the head trimmer and add some facial hair. In this way, you can wear your new look with confidence. The alternative is a comb-over, which tells the world you're losing your confidence as well as your hair.

WHAT TO DO WITH YOUR FACE

It's very important to look after your skin. It's the largest organ you have, weighing six times as much as your liver in second place. Of all your organs, it's also the most visible. Let's start with how to shave properly and then look at the face products available to keep us looking silky smooth (we'll come back to facial hair in a minute).

SHAVE LIKE A MAN

I'm going to assume that we all know how to use an electric shaver and move right along to the manlier option of getting blade on skin. If this is already a ritual for you, but you haven't given it much thought lately, the following advice might just rejuvenate your face.

The pre-shave: always shower first if you can. This softens the bristles ready for shaving and makes sure you're wide awake before putting a sharp blade in the vicinity of your jugular vein. If you can't shower first, apply copious amounts of hot water to your face instead. Either way, apply pre-shave oil or ointment to ensure a smooth shaving experience.

The lather: whether you apply cream or gel by hand, or soap or cream by brush, apply it for at least 10 seconds to work it properly into your face. Using a brush and shaving soap is best to achieve a deep level of penetration, and it also makes you look extra manly should your partner or date suddenly walk into the bathroom. Always use a lather appropriate to your skin type, especially if you have sensitive skin.

The brush: nothing but badger hair will do if you want the best, and nothing but 'super badger' will do if you want the very best. If you are ever tempted to pluck a badger yourself, 'super badger' is the very fine silver-tipped hair that can be found on the badger's neck. If, on the other hand, you are more concerned about the welfare of badgers than the quality of your shaving brush, synthetic-bristled brushes are available.

The razor: there is a bewildering choice of cutthroat, safety and multi-blade safety out there. If you have sensitive skin and want to avoid scraping four or five blades across it every morning, or if you want to feel a bit more Crocodile Dundee but can't go the whole cutthroat, go for the double-edged single blade that you pop into the top of the razor.

The shave: always use a sharp blade and let it do the work. Light, short strokes in the direction of the growth will do a reasonable job. If you want a really close shave (on the morning of your wedding, say), finish by shaving across or against the grain, but be careful doing this if you have sensitive skin – the ensuing rash could leave your face looking more like a badger's bottom than a badger's brush.

The post-shave: rinse your face thoroughly with warm water to remove excess lather and finish with a cold rinse to close the pores against the rigours of everyday life. Then moisturise and apply aftershave lotion (but don't overdo this, because it will make you smell as if you're trying just a little too hard and no one wants a desperate man).

GROOMING HACK

If you're not comfortable trying to get a super-clean shave by yourself and you need to look your best for a date, wedding or other special occasion, go to a proper barber and treat yourself to a wet shave with a cutthroat razor. You'll feel smooth and fresh and your barber will have the kind of products that will leave you smelling pretty good too.

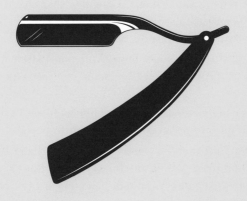

FACIAL HAIR

You're either into facial hair or you're not. If you're not sure, you can easily find out by experimenting a bit. You will either like yourself with facial hair or you won't, and your partner, friends and family won't be slow in telling you what they think either. The choices are 'designer' stubble, moustache, beard only, or the 'full set' of moustache and beard, and there are many variations on each of those options to put to trial and error. However, there are some rules you should bear in mind:

- Give a new moustache and/or beard a good four to six weeks to get going in order to ensure full, even growth.
- Buying a multi-grooming kit will give you different combs that allow you to experiment with different lengths of facial hair.
- Don't have your beard similar in length or shape to your hairstyle, because people will stare at you while they try to figure out whether your head would look just the same upside down.
- Don't forget to trim your eyebrows from time to time with a beard trimmer or, if you don't have one, some small scissors will have to do to.
- Invest in combined nose and ear trimmers to get to the bits that you really don't want to take a sharp blade to.
- Trimming your eyebrows and nose and ear hairs is especially important if you're getting on a bit, because nothing says 'old man' more than unkempt eyebrows or hairs hanging out of your nose or ears.

FACIAL PRODUCTS

Whether you have facial hair or not, it's important to understand which of the many facial products on offer are right for you. Trial and error once more come into play, but do bear the following in mind:

- Use beard shampoo when washing your beard, as ordinary hair shampoo will strip away the natural oils in your skin.

- A microfibre face cloth is a gentler option to dry your face after shaving or trimming, because regular towels tend to pull at your roots.

- Apply a good-quality moisturiser after trimming. Beard balms are good to keep thick beards looking and feeling healthy and beard oils are great for conditioning shorter beards. Whichever you use, remember to work it into the skin below.

- Post-shave moisturisers will claim to have miracle properties that do everything from the prevention of redness on your skin to the slowing down of the ageing process. They will tell you that these miracles are made possible by the inclusion of sandalwood, citrus fruits, botanicals, cedar, baobab, blue alpine thistle and much more besides. Just find one that works for you and that you like the smell of.

GROOMING YOUR
OTHER BODY PARTS

With all this talk of hair and faces, it would be easy to forget about the other opportunities open to the committed self-groomer. Here are some options to get you thinking:

Mani-pedi: the man's mani and the man's pedi are often offered as a package at the many salons that are now catering for men in what was long regarded as women-only territory. You will leave with great nails and smoother skin on both your hands and feet, and the associated massage will add to an increased confidence in your handshake and a rejuvenated spring in your step.

Back treatment: a massage will release muscle tension and the deep cleansing of the parts you can't reach in the shower will ensure that you are clean all over.

Manscaping: this does what the name suggests, in that it tidies up whichever parts of your landscape need tidying up, including your eyebrows, chest, back, arms and legs, and even your more private parts. Much of it you can do at home if you have the time and the right trimmers and, when it comes to down below, if you have a steady enough hand and a nerve that will hold long enough to complete the job (let's be honest, it's not the best place to nick yourself with a razor). If you can afford it, though, salons will do it quicker and better for you, especially if you opt for removal by waxing. Hair removal creams are also available for the more squeamish among us.

Smoothing out the cracks: if you want to go the whole hog and have the inside of your backside done, please don't try it at home with a wet razor. It would be much quicker to throw yourself off a tall building. Instead, get it waxed professionally, but only if you have a high pain threshold!

MALE BODY FACTS

- According to a 2017 study carried out by a medical journal, 67 per cent of men have carried out some manscaping 'down there'. This may to some extent be down to the fact that the removal of pubic hair creates the illusion of an extra inch or so.

- If you removed all your skin and stretched it out flat, it would cover about 1.85 sq m (20 sq ft).

- You have around 100,000–150,000 hairs on your scalp alone (unless you're bald of course).

- Beards have the fastest-growing hairs on the male body, with the average male growing about 25,000 facial hairs every 24 hours.

STYLISH TRIVIA

Here are some great stylish facts to get you set up for the day:

The reason we have decorative buttons on jacket sleeves is that Napoleon got fed up with his snotty soldiers wiping their runny noses on their sleeves.

Neckties are the most common Father's Day gift worldwide.

Panama hats have never been made in Panama. The nineteenth-century hat makers of Ecuador just decided to take their hats up to Panama to take advantage of its passing trade through the canal. Wherever the hat buyers went in the world, people asked them where they got their nice hats. 'Panama,' they said.

Denim jeans are not as American as you might think. When Levi Strauss set about clothing the gold-diggers, cowboys and railroad builders of the Wild West, the strongest fabric he could find was *serge de Nîmes* in France. So denim was just pioneer speak for *de Nîmes*.

In North Korea, jeans and piercings are banned on the grounds that they are too capitalist, and people have to choose from a state-sanctioned list of haircuts. If men really want to curry favour, they can go for the roadkill-perched-on-top-of-the-head style sported by dictator Kim Jong-un.

NOTES ON THE MALE UNDERCARRIAGE

If you're at all squeamish about the bits you have dangling down below, look away now, or at least make sure your door is locked before you start checking out the following observations on the male anatomy:

You really need to know which side you naturally hang towards, because it's only a matter of time before a tailor will ask you 'On which side does sir dress?' for the purposes of bespoking you the perfect trouser crotch.

Unless you favour the 'lunchbox' look made famous by Lycra-clad sprinters (and you really shouldn't), always leave a bit of breathing space when choosing shorts or trousers.

Squeeze yourself regularly down there: if you remember nothing else you read in this book, remember this – advanced testicular cancer is not something you want and checking your own testicles for lumps or other changes once a month after a shower is the best way to alleviate fear or alert you to any potential problem. The sooner you have any irregularities checked out, the better. Just do it.

THE MANLY WAY TO TRAVEL AND SEEK ADVENTURE

Whether you're an adrenaline junkie or just a natural-born explorer, this chapter has tips on how to get the most out of your travels. It will tell you how to stay alive in the great outdoors and how to be manly in Manly (it's in Australia, if you don't know), and it will suggest some great trips by road, rail and foot. If you're into proper hard adventure travel, you can drool over the possibilities in the 'Rugged bucket list'.

GREAT TRAILS TO HIKE

If it's fresh air and exercise you're after, get your walking boots on and try some of the world's great paths, which include the following:

Inca Trail (Peru): allow four days to hike the 42 km (26 miles) of gruelling inclines and declines at altitude. You will be rewarded with the magnificent sight of Machu Picchu at the end, though.

Mount Kilimanjaro (Tanzania): Kilimanjaro is the tallest freestanding mountain on earth and its altitude has defeated many otherwise fit climbers. It takes six or seven very slow and often painful days to scale the 5,894 m (19,340 ft), but you do get to gaze down on Africa.

Petra (Jordan): an 80-km (50-mile) trek south from Dana over five to nine days, sleeping under the desert sky in Bedouin tents. The end destination, of course, is epic, offering up the temples and tombs of the ancient Red Rose City of Petra.

Milford Track (New Zealand): the most popular of the many amazing hiking options in the Fiordland National Park on South Island. Running from the head of Lake Te Anau to the beautiful Milford Sound, you will traverse rainforest, wetlands and alpine passes.

Pacific Crest Trail (USA): now that you're warmed up, it's time to tackle this 4,265-km (2,650-mile) track through California, Oregon and Washington. Allow at least six months to take in the seven national parks along the way and be prepared to tackle everything from 3,962-m (13,000-ft) climbs to the heat of the Mojave Desert.

INSPIRATIONAL ADVENTURERS

From Christopher Columbus to Neil Armstrong, some men just can't ever seem to get enough of exploration or adventure. Let's take a look at two awe-inspiring examples of our own time:

RANULPH FIENNES

After serving as a demolition expert in the SAS and being awarded a medal for bravery fighting for the Sultan of Oman, Fiennes went on to be recognised by Guinness World Records as the 'World's Greatest Living Explorer'. He has travelled from pole to pole, crossed the Antarctic on foot unsupported, was part of the team that discovered the lost city of Ubar in the Omani desert and overcame vertigo to climb Mount Everest at the ripe old age of 65. After one Arctic expedition, the tips of his fingers on one hand were so severely frostbitten that he cut them off in his garden shed to avoid the wait for surgery.

He remains the only man alive to have travelled around the world's circumpolar surface (the vertical equivalent of walking round the equator, but with lots more frostbite), and just four months after a double heart bypass operation he ran seven marathons in seven days on the seven different geographical continents of the world (although the Falklands had to substitute for Antarctica after bad weather forced a rerouting).

ARON RALSTON

In 2003, mountain climber Aron Ralston was descending a narrow canyon in Utah when a boulder slipped and trapped his right hand against a rock face. Having tried unsuccessfully for three days to pull his arm free, he decided to amputate the lower part of his forearm with the small blade of his pocketknife, but it was too blunt to cut through bone.

Becoming delirious and reduced to drinking his own urine by day five, he hit upon the idea of breaking the bones in his arm by snapping them between the boulder and the rock face, which he duly did. This allowed him to cut through the gaps in his bones in about an hour, following which he abseiled down the remainder of the rock and began the 8-km (5-mile) hike back to his truck. He stumbled upon some tourists, who alerted the emergency services, who airlifted him to hospital within four hours of his DIY amputation.

At the time of his accident, Ralston had been working his way through Colorado's 'fourteeners' – 53 mountains over 4,267 m (14,000 ft). Undaunted by his little mishap in Utah, he climbed the final three in 2005, becoming the first person to climb the lot solo and in winter.

He is now an inspirational speaker, encouraging others to overcome adversity in life. So, the next time you feel a bit down in the dumps, break your own arm, cut a bit of it off and crack on with your life. It's the manly thing to do.

Note: you can read the full story in Ralston's 2004 book *Between a Rock and a Hard Place*, or watch it unfold in the 2010 Danny Boyle movie *127 Hours*.

GREAT TRAIN RIDES

It's hard to beat the thrill of travelling on foreign trains, especially when they take you through geography that is inaccessible to motor cars.

GLACIER EXPRESS (SWITZERLAND)

Glacier Express is something of a misnomer as it takes 8 hours to cover the spectacular 290 km (180 miles) between Zermatt and St Moritz in the Swiss Alps, but it's still quicker than walking across 291 ravines to reach your ski resort.

OSLO–BERGEN LINE (NORWAY)

Enjoy the sight of oxblood wooden cabins dotted around crystal-clear fjords and, if you can, add the spectacular branch-line excursion from Myrdal down to Flåm, which drops 863 m (2,831 ft) over 20 km (12.5 miles) to Sognefjord, Norway's longest and deepest fjord.

EASTERN & ORIENTAL EXPRESS (SOUTH EAST ASIA)

The European cities you can still visit in expensive luxury on the Orient Express today include London, Paris, Venice, Stockholm and Vienna. For something a little sultrier, the Eastern & Oriental Express allows you to have a similar (but smart-casual) experience on the 1,931-km (1,200-mile) Bangkok–Kuala Lumpur–Singapore line.

'TOY TRAIN' TO DARJEELING (INDIAN HIMALAYAS)

Take the narrow-gauge Darjeeling Himalayan Railway, popularly known as the 'Toy Train', for just a fistful of rupees. Clouds permitting, you will get a panoramic view that includes Mounts Everest and Kangchenjunga, two of the world's three highest mountains.

SHOSHOLOZA MEYL (SOUTH AFRICA)

Forget about the luxury Blue Train and Rovos Rail services and travel the 1,530 km (950 miles) between Cape Town and Johannesburg on the public Shosholoza Meyl sleeper service for a fraction of the price. The endless savannah, wild animals and stunning sunsets will be the same, making this the biggest rail-travel bargain you are ever likely to strike in your entire life.

TRANS-SIBERIAN RAILWAY (RUSSIA AND CHINA)

For a fraction of the cost of the luxury Golden Eagle service, the state-run *Rossiya* ('Russia') service will carry you the same 9,900 km (6,152 miles) over eight days and seven time zones to conquer Siberia and reach Vladivostok on the Sea of Japan. If you can afford it, there is also a Moscow–Beijing alternative serviced by a Chinese train, the Trans-Mongolian Express.

AUCKLAND–WELLINGTON NORTHERN EXPLORER (NEW ZEALAND)

It takes 11 hours to cross the 680 km (423 miles) of North Island that separates New Zealand's two largest cities. You won't tire of the ever-changing scenery and might see hobbit holes as you pass through the territory used as the Shire in *The Lord of the Rings* and *The Hobbit* movies.

ROCKY MOUNTAINEER (CANADA)

The most famous Rocky Mountaineer trip is the First Passage to the West, the route that runs over the original Canadian Pacific track between Vancouver and Banff. Even by Canadian standards the mountain scenery is hard to beat and the stops include spectacular Lake Louise.

GREAT ROAD TRIPS

If you're like me and like nothing more than a road trip, consider the following when booking your next fly-drive:

California State Route 1 (USA): drive the portion that has San Francisco at one end and Los Angeles at the other and you will get to enjoy Santa Barbara, Carmel and Monterey along the way. If you have time, take side trips to Las Vegas and as many National Parks as you can (possibilities include Grand Canyon, Yosemite, Death Valley and Joshua Tree).

Garden Route (South Africa): drive the 515 km (320 miles) from Cape Town to Plettenberg Bay for wonderful views combined with opportunities to whale watch, dive with great white sharks and take a Big Five safari. And don't even get me started on the wine tasting.

South Island (New Zealand): you can follow a roughly rectangular route around the entire island to enjoy the huge variety of stunning scenery that is stuffed into this relatively small geographical area. Take as much time as you can to explore some of the many lakes, mountains and fiords that can be discovered by taking side trips inland or towards the coastline.

North Coast 500 (Scotland): most of the 805-km (500-mile) route along Scotland's north coast is winding and much of it is single track. Slow progress is exactly what you want, though, to appreciate the extraordinary scenery replete with haunting castles and whisky distilleries.

GREAT CYCLE RIDES

If you like a bit more exercise on holiday, consider adding the following to your bucket list:

Route 66: take a week to do the 423 km (263 miles) from Flagstaff, Arizona to Las Vegas, Nevada. Enjoy challenging climbs, wonderfully long descents and a finishing line on the Vegas Strip.

Saddle safari in Tanzania: allow 11 days for the 467 km (290 miles) from Arusha (West Kilimanjaro) to Pangani Town on the Indian Ocean. You will see Mount Kilimanjaro, colourful Masai villages and more wildlife than you ever thought possible from a saddle.

The Dubai desert: cycle the 85-km (53-mile) Al Qudra Bike Track (known as 'the Lollipop' on account of its shape). Glass-smooth tarmac takes you through the desert with ease as long as you avoid the midday sun and dust storms.

Vietnam to Laos: eight days should cover the 507 km (315 miles) from Hanoi in Vietnam to Luang Prabang in neighbouring Laos. It's mostly a mixture of flat and downhill, but you need a reasonable level of fitness to cope with the heat and humidity. Expect to see saffron-clad monks, paddy fields and gilded temples.

Tasmania's Mount Wellington: ride like the (Tasmanian) devil from the top of the mountain to the city of Hobart below. It's a descent over 21 km (13 miles) which will last for about two and a half hours. Feel free to also tackle the climb, although the average 6–9 per cent gradient and the rough surface do make it a bit gruelling.

TRAVEL QUOTES

LIVE IN THE SUNSHINE, SWIM IN THE SEA, DRINK THE WILD AIR.

Ralph Waldo Emerson

• • • • • • • • • •

BUT MY LIFE WAS TOO SHORT TO ACHIEVE THE CONQUEST OF THE WORLD. THAT TASK IS LEFT FOR YOU.

Genghis Khan, exhorting men everywhere
to have a gap year (following his own
success at laying waste to Europe and
Asia in the thirteenth century)

TRAVEL JOKES

I ALWAYS WRITE MY JOKES IN CAPITALS. I WROTE THIS ONE IN PARIS.

• • • • • • • • •

PEOPLE WHO USE SELFIE STICKS SHOULD HAVE A LONG, HARD LOOK AT THEMSELVES.

ADRENALINE-FUELLED ACTIVITIES

If you think ordinary travelling is for the faint-hearted, you might want to consider the following crazy stuff:

Fatbiking: the wide, deep-tread tyres of fatbikes let you cycle on snow, frozen lakes, riverbanks or sand dunes. Used for commuting in the northernmost parts of the world, but just as popular with adventure seekers anywhere the environment is too tricky even for mountain bikes.

Skydiving: if you're up for it, go for the HALO (high altitude, low open). This military-style dive will have you freefalling at 322 kph (200 mph). If money isn't an object, you can choose to skydive at the North Pole or over Mount Everest or the pyramids of Egypt.

Bungee jumping: you can jump off some of the world's travel hotspots, including the Victoria Falls Bridge on the border of Zambia and Zimbabwe, but you can also do it from a helicopter or hot-air balloon if you find jumping from a fixed object a little claustrophobic.

Sandboarding: like snowboarding but on sand dunes instead of snow. The speeds you reach are exhilarating but the landings if you fall are soft. It's happening all around the world, but the Sahara Desert must be the biggest trophy to have on your sandboarding CV.

White-water rafting: choose from tumbling down glacier-fed mountain rivers (think Alaska) or those that wind down through Amazonian rainforests. Or combine the two environments by starting up in the Himalayas and rafting down to the tropical jungle that surrounds the Ganges in India.

GREAT WILD SWIMS

If you can't resist the lure of water and want to combine it with the very best that nature has to offer, try some wild swimming at locations like these:

Yukatán sinkholes (Mexico): natural limestone sinkholes known as cenotes offer icy dips in turquoise pools.

Blue Cave (Croatia): this grotto on the island of Biševo turns royal blue when sunlight penetrates the cave in the middle of the day.

Pelican Bar (Jamaica): take a boat out to this rickety old bar and swim off the surrounding sand bars. If you're lucky, some dolphins might join you.

Crystal River (USA): this waterway in Florida lives up to its name because the water is in fact crystal clear. It is also home to gentle manatees and you are allowed to swim with them.

Fraser Island (Australia): the world's largest sand island offers idyllic swimming opportunities, but the waters can get a bit 'sharky' and there are also some resident crocs, so be sure to take local advice about where to swim. Or at least be lucky.

→ GOING BALLISTIC ←

If budget isn't an issue and you just can't get enough adrenaline pumping through your veins on Mother Earth, I recommend booking a Virgin Galactic space flight for US$250,000. The first flights should be happening soon, although Virgin Galactic has been saying that for a while now.

Alternatively, keep costs down to US$20,000 with a MiGFlug supersonic, edge-of-space flight from Russia in a MiG-29 jet fighter. You will be treated to rolls, loops and vertical climbs and dives at almost Mach 2. If I were you, I'd stick to a light breakfast that day.

HACKING YOUR WAY AROUND THE WORLD'S CITIES

Most people with a smartphone are accustomed to using a map to navigate around towns and cities, but that can be costly if you're abroad and can't rely on a consistent Internet connection. The best way to overcome this is to download a map app that works offline.

There are now plenty to choose from and they'll all have the same functions as your favourite online map app. They'll point out bars, restaurants and other points of interest, and they'll allow you to 'pin' desired destinations for easy navigation later.

You just can't go wrong with this one!

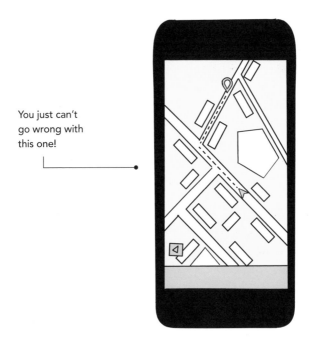

HACK YOUR WAY TO BETTER INSTAGRAM PHOTOS

In order to instil wonder and even envy in your Instagram followers, follow these four simple rules:

For soft, natural lighting, take advantage of the 'golden hours' by taking photographs in the hour following sunrise and the hour leading up to sunset.

Stop preening about and focus on the beauty of your surroundings. Play a minor part in the photo if you must, but nobody wants to see your face all the time.

Try to find some blue to include in your photos (sky and sea are prime candidates, so are blue clothes). Because the colour is associated with holiday calm and relaxation, photos that contain some blue get around 25 per cent more 'likes' than photos with other colours in them.

Go filter-free as much as you can, because people prefer a natural, believable image and they'll usually be able to tell if you've been 'cheating'.

TRAVEL TRIVIA

You might like to bear in mind the following random pieces of trivia just in case they pop up in some quiz or other:

Australia's Great Barrier Reef stretches 3,000 km (1,800 miles) alongside the coast of Queensland and is the only living structure on earth visible from space.

The Shire village of Hobbiton in *The Lord of the Rings* and *The Hobbit* movies was located in the farming area of Matamata on New Zealand's North Island and remains there as a tourist attraction.

To counter the effects of air pollution, you can buy cans of fresh air in China, including cans of Canadian, Australian and Tibetan air.

The Maldives are only on average 1.2 m (4 ft) above the waters of the Indian Ocean and scientists think the island republic might disappear altogether within 60 years. Go there now if you can.

The Chinese New Year is responsible for the largest human migration on earth each year. Almost 3 billion people undertake journeys home by plane, train, car, motorcycle and bicycle.

It is estimated that two-thirds of people in the world have never seen snow.

Rainbows are circular. We can only see the top half from ground level, but you can sometimes see a whole rainbow from a plane or even a mountaintop.

BUCKET LISTS FOR THE ADVENTURE SEEKER

THE RUGGED BUCKET LIST

If you're thinking about doing some hard adventure travelling, on a gap year maybe, it might help to draw up a personal bucket list. Here are some suggestions to get you going.

- Trek the 65 km (40 miles) from Lukla in Nepal to Mount Everest South Base Camp. You will climb up to 5,364 m (17,598 ft) above sea level, which is well over halfway to the top of the mountain.
- Cross the world's largest dry desert, the Sahara, by camel or truck – I recommend doing so on a north–south basis, which keeps the distance down to a manageable 1,800 km (1,118 miles), which is especially helpful if you choose the camel option.
- Swim in the world's largest lake, the Caspian Sea. If you wanted to swim around its entire 7,000-km (4,300-mile) perimeter, you would take in the waters of Russia, Kazakhstan, Turkmenistan, Iran and Azerbaijan – I have taken the liberty here of assuming you prefer to swim round huge lakes in a clockwise direction.
- Travel the Pan-American Highway, the world's longest at 30,000 km (19,000 miles). It runs north–south from Alaska to Chile and the only snag is the 102-km (66-mile) Darién Gap straddling Panama and Colombia, where a mixture of rainforest and swamp doesn't lend itself to roadbuilding (so either you need an all-terrain vehicle or a quick detour by sea).
- Rent a dhow and sail along as much as you can of the 6,695 km (4,160 miles) of the world's longest river, the Nile. It will offer you selfie opportunities along the shorelines of up to 11 different African countries.

- Jump off the world's highest bungee platform, which is the deck of a glass-bottomed bridge across the Zhangjiajie Grand Canyon in China. The landing area is 260 m (850 ft) down, but don't worry, it won't take long to reach it.

THE NOT-SO-RUGGED BUCKET LIST

If, on the other hand, you want a bucket list that's a bit less challenging but is still pretty cool, try the following:

- Walk across the world's smallest country, the Vatican City. It is 0.85 km (0.53 miles) wide, so about ten minutes should do it.
- Drive round the Monaco Grand Prix circuit in your own car at legal speeds on any day of the year it isn't being used by racing cars, which is most days of the year. The circuit is just over 3.4 km (2 miles), so each 'lap' will only take you a few minutes.
- Float in the Dead Sea in Jordan or Israel, the deepest depression on the earth's surface at 408 m (1,338 ft) below sea level.
- Drive the world's hottest drive, Death Valley in California, which boasts temperatures of up to 56.7°C (134°F).
- Ride on the Shanghai Maglev, the world's fastest, commercial, high-speed electric train. It only takes 7 minutes 20 seconds to travel the 30 km (18.6 miles) between Shanghai Pudong International Airport and Longyang Road station.
- Travel to the world's most popular tourist destination, which is France. While there, you can take in the Louvre in Paris, the world's most-visited museum.
- Catch a plane to the most-visited tourist attraction in the world, which is the Las Vegas Strip in Nevada, USA.

TRAVEL TIPS

There are lots of websites to advise you on the dos and don'ts of travel, but here are just some of my favourites to smooth your path into the big, wide world:

Always have some emergency cash on you. A leather money belt looks just like a belt and the zip at the back lets you stash away a few rolled-up notes.

Keep sand off your phone and hide your valuables out of sight by putting them in plastic containers that look like suntan bottles (they're widely available on Amazon and many other online sites).

Splash out on a new waterproof Kindle (see what I did there?) and spend your holidays reading on pool inflatables.

Get yourself a Starling or Monzo debit card for your travels. Within a second of using it anywhere in the world in whichever currency, it will send an alert to your phone telling you how much you just spent in the foreign currency and in your home currency. It will also categorise how much you are spending on what to help with your holiday budgeting. Indispensable on a gap year.

THINGS NOT TO DO ON YOUR TRAVELS

There are some weird things you can't do on your travels, because they're illegal, sometimes for good reason, sometimes because no one ever got around to removing them from the statute books. Either way, here are some of the things you can't do.

- Shoot a buffalo from the second storey of a hotel in Texas.
- Fall off the top of the Blackpool Tower in the UK.
- Complain about the lack of light during the long hours of winter in Sweden.
- Urinate in the ocean in Portugal (although I'm pretty sure you can get away with this using just a small amount of discretion).
- Dance naked at an ancient site in Greece (if you're really determined, perhaps do it at night, but be wary of any barbed-wire fences).
- Fly a UFO over Châteauneuf-du-Pape in France.
- Ride a cow while drunk in Scotland.
- Fly a kite to the annoyance of another person in Australia.
- Drive while under the influence of drink in El Salvador. No different to anywhere else really, except the sentence if you're caught is to face death by firing squad.
- Chew gum in Singapore (hefty fines for first and second offences, hard labour thereafter).

GET MANLY IN MANLY

This destination in Sydney's Northern Beaches is surely the manliest-sounding place a man could travel to! There also happens to be a Manly in Iowa, USA, but there isn't much to do when you get there (according to the town's own Facebook page, there are 'No recommended places to see'). In the Manly that is Down Under, however, there is a whole lot of manly stuff to do when you get there, including the following:

- Swim, surf, snorkel, kayak or paddle-board in shark-infested waters (and, if needs be, get yourself rescued by the Manly Life Saving Club).
- Walk or cycle the Manly Scenic Walkway to Shelly Beach, keeping an eye open for water dragons on the rocks and whales, dolphins and penguins in the adjacent water.
- Play volleyball on Manly Beach, the birthplace of Australian beach volleyball.
- Take a selfie standing next to any road sign or shopfront or bus stop that contains the word 'Manly'.
- Watch Manly United play soccer, Manly RUFC play rugby union or Manly Warringah Sea Eagles play rugby league.
- If you're feeling romantic and you normally hang out in the northern hemisphere, get married on Manly Beach in the middle of winter (because it will, of course, be summer there).
- Catch the Manly ferry that runs regularly between Manly Wharf and Circular Quay in Sydney, and when you get there climb the world-famous 'Coathanger', aka Sydney Harbour Bridge (but be sure to book in advance, because it's a very popular attraction).

OTHER MANLY PLACES TO VISIT AROUND THE WORLD

If you've become hooked on manly selfies after snapping yourself in front of a Manly sign in New South Wales or Iowa, here are ten other manly sounding places around the world that you should travel to in order to put together a collage of selfies that will be the envy of your less peripatetic friends.

1. Batman, Turkey
2. Gnaw Bone, Indiana
3. Condom, France
4. Longpole, West Virginia
5. Beer, Devon (England)
6. Hell, Michigan
7. Shag Point, New Zealand
8. Great Snoring, Norfolk (England)
9. Rough and Ready, California (and there's another one in Pennsylvania)
10. Dull, Scottish Highlands

Note: Dull has been twinned with Boring, Oregon in the USA and Bland Shire in Australia to form the 'League of Extraordinary Communities'. Their signs might not be very manly, but any selfies taken in front of them will contain self-deprecating humour, which will show that you're pretty cool in addition to being just the right amount of macho.

TRAVEL QUOTES

IF YOU THINK ADVENTURE IS DANGEROUS, TRY ROUTINE; IT'S LETHAL.

Paulo Coelho

• • • • • • • • •

I MUCH PREFER TRAVELLING IN NON-BRITISH SHIPS. THERE'S NONE OF THAT NONSENSE ABOUT WOMEN AND CHILDREN FIRST.

Somerset Maugham

TRAVEL JOKES

A HOTEL MINIBAR ALLOWS YOU TO LOOK INTO THE FUTURE AND SEE WHAT A BOTTLE OF WATER WILL COST IN 2050.

• • • • • • • • •

INTERESTED IN TIME TRAVEL?
MEET HERE LAST THURSDAY AT 7 P.M.

• • • • • • • • •

I WENT ON A ONCE-IN-A-LIFETIME HOLIDAY. NEVER AGAIN.

TIPS ON HOW TO STAY ALIVE IN THE GREAT OUTDOORS (PART ONE)

Here are some useful tips (or reminders if you're already an experienced outdoorsman) on how to prevent or recover from difficult situations:

1. Educate yourself about survival techniques by reading one of the many books available on the subject, especially if you intend to go into the wild alone. At the very least, make sure you understand the following:

- Which clothes to wear in which environment.
- How to build (and start) a fire.
- The basics of orientation and navigation using the stars and/or a compass.
- The need to check weather forecasts.
- How to live off the land, e.g. know which vegetation is edible and which is not.
- How to administer first aid on yourself or your fellow outdoorsmen and, in particular, how to manufacture a splint for a damaged limb.
- The need to tell at least two other people where you are going and how to contact you if they don't hear from you by a certain time or day.
- The need to attain the level of physical fitness appropriate for your intended activities.

2. Never leave home or base camp without the following items:

- Your mobile phone (cellphone)
- A back-up phone battery
- Emergency contact details (laminated)
- A compass and a waterproof map
- Water and purifiers
- Protein bars and dried fruit
- Matches in a sealed bag or a lighter of sorts
- Waterproof bivouac or sleeping bag
- First-aid pack
- Multipurpose knife (e.g. Swiss Army knife)
- Torch and spare batteries
- Duct tape for running repairs

3. If you do get into trouble, bear in mind the following advice:

- Don't panic. Take deep breaths while you assess your situation and think through the steps you would advise someone else to take in the same situation.
- Begin immediately to ration what food and water you have in case you need to keep yourself hydrated and nourished for longer than you originally provisioned for.
- If you can, find water from a stream or river and use your water purifiers to make it safe to drink.
- Stand your ground if you find yourself face to face with a wild animal. Make yourself as big as possible to send the message that it should be more afraid of you than you are of it. Running away will simply bring out the predator in it. If all else fails, play dead.

TIPS ON HOW TO STAY ALIVE IN THE GREAT OUTDOORS (PART TWO)

In addition to following the advice in part one, also bear in mind these tips about some of the wild animals or fish you might come across on your travels:

The friendly sounding **honey badger** is in fact the 'World's Most Fearless Creature' according to Guinness World Records. It will fight any other creature it comes across to the death, including lions, hyenas, leopards, pythons and your hand should you choose to stroke it.

By all means watch out for **crocodiles** as you travel the world, but also be aware that hippos and buffalo both kill more people than crocodiles do. If you get between them and their watering holes, there will only be one winner.

A **shark** can detect one part of blood in a million parts of water, but statisticians regularly point out that you are more likely to be killed by a falling coconut. That is why I hope sharks evolve the ability to detect one part of a statistician's blood anywhere on land or water.

The black-and-white **killer whale**, or orca, eats its way through everything it comes across in the ocean, including octopuses, dolphins, seals, penguins, sharks and other whales. It will also help itself to land-based mammals, like reindeer (and you) swimming between islands.

The **red-bellied piranha** of South America will eat anything, including cattle or tourists who stoop to have a drink in the wrong river at the wrong time. They will have your hand, nose and mouth as a starter and carry on from there.

If you ever find yourself being chased by a **tiger**, try not to dwell on the fact that it can run at 64 kph (40 mph) and swim for up to 32 km (20 miles). Unless, of course, you're a triathlete, in which case just enjoy the challenge for as long as it lasts.

The **Tasmanian devil** is a violent mammal with a small body and a large head. Even Australians give it a wide berth and they surf in shark-infested waters.

The **tapir** of South and Central America looks like a large pig with a small trunk, but it's apparently related to the rhinoceros, so you might not want to call it a large pig with a small trunk to its face.

The **green anaconda** of South America doesn't need venom, because it's big enough to swallow pigs, caimans, jaguars and human beings whole. Avoid the green anaconda.

The **wolverine** of northern Europe, Canada and Alaska looks like a cross between a skunk and a bear. It doesn't therefore bear much resemblance to Hugh Jackman, but it is every bit as fierce as his *X-Men* character, so don't go near it.

GREAT CAMPING SPOTS AROUND THE WORLD

There are countless great camping spots around the world, of course, but here are just four prime examples to illustrate the variety available to you:

Abel Tasman National Park (New Zealand): pitch up here and your neighbours will include bellbirds, little blue penguins and fur seals. The environment is a mixture of coastal waters, sandy beaches and forest.

Florida Keys (USA): there are many campsites to choose from along the 38 keys (islands) that stretch out from the tip of mainland Florida. All accessible by the same 182-km (113-mile) Overseas Highway, the keys offer sandy beaches and waterborne activities aplenty.

Maasai Mara National Reserve (Kenya): go on a safari with a difference with only your guide and cook for company, and only a tent between you and the animals outside. You will hear everything there is to hear in the dead of night, quite possibly including the uncomfortable sounds of prey being hunted down and ripped apart.

Snowdonia National Park (Wales): try your hand at wild camping anywhere within the park, but do understand your own capabilities and limitations, and make sure you check the weather forecast before deciding on an open or sheltered spot for the night. The sunset and sunrise will be almost spiritual if you choose the right night.

MANLY HEALTH AND HAPPINESS

There is nothing more important than staying healthy and happy, but the fast pace of twenty-first-century life can sometimes make it difficult for us to find the time and energy to exercise properly or eat the right things or even just stay positive. This chapter looks at the ways we can exercise, from high-intensity interval training (HIIT) sessions at the gym to exercises we can do while sitting in front of the TV. It also offers some tips on what to eat when, and what we can do to remain positive enough to feed our mind, body and soul the happiness they deserve.

MEN WHO INSPIRE THE MIND, BODY AND SOUL

Some men become enlightened about a better way forward for the human race and are able to articulate it in such a way that it gains a following that can last for generations:

Gautama Buddha (fifth century BC): the monk and sage whose teachings led to the foundation of Buddhism. He taught a 'Middle Way' between the self-indulgence and self-deprivation teachings of others.

Joseph Pilates (1883–1967): after suffering from asthma, rheumatic fever and rickets as a child growing up in Germany, Pilates made it his life's mission to help himself and others strengthen their muscles and improve their posture, flexibility and stamina.

Tirumalai Krishnamacharya (1888–1989): the Indian yogi, healer and health expert is hailed as the 'father of modern yoga' because he was the first to combine breathing and movement in his teachings.

Zheng Ji (1900–2010): the Chinese founder and professor of nutrition studies proved his point by living until he was 110.

Dalai Lama (1935–): the spiritual leader of the Tibetan people is also a prolific author and speaker who is devoted to helping the world achieve mental and spiritual health – 19 million Twitter followers can't be wrong.

HEALTHY DAY-TO-DAY ACTIVITIES

There are some things you can do to stay fit and healthy without signing up for a gym membership or shelling out for expensive equipment or gadgets. You just have to do them. Here are some examples:

Drink at least 2 litres of water a day: only then can every cell, tissue and organ in your body maintain their proper temperature, flush out what they don't need and lubricate your joints. This is especially important if you're going to be working out or playing sport, of course.

Don't sit when you can stand: if you have to sit to do your job, make sure you stand up and move around or stretch, however briefly, every 20 minutes. Purpose-built standing desks are also becoming increasingly popular and there are even adjustable-height ones that allow you to mix sitting and standing throughout the working day.

HACKING YOUR WAY TO BETTER POSTURE

If you want to try out working at your PC while standing up, just pile up some sturdy boxes or coffee-table books under your equipment until you're looking down slightly on the middle of your screen and your keyboard and mouse/trackpad are at elbow height.

Don't sit or stand when you can walk: whether or not your general aim is to achieve the trending 10,000 steps a day on your Fitbit, try to walk whenever you can. Get off the bus or train at an earlier stop and walk the rest of the way home or to the office; go for a brisk stroll around your neighbourhood in the evening instead of slumping in front of the TV; and always take the stairs if possible – the elevator is your enemy.

Don't walk slowly when you can walk fast: speed walking is becoming very popular as a way to keep fit going about your normal day. You would be surprised how much faster you can walk from A to B by just looking as if you're late for a train or a meeting.

Park further away: easy ways to get a bit of added exercise are to park at the far end of the supermarket car park or 5–10 minutes away from the cinema, high street, doctor/dentist or anywhere else you need to go.

Don't walk when you can cycle: get out that old bike and pump up the tyres and check the brakes. It will be great for short trips to the nearby shops or to catch a train from your local station.

Exercise at home: you can do anything from a full workout to a few stretches in the comfort of your own home. Yoga also works and even dancing to MTV is great exercise if you have the house to yourself (or if your partner is also a bit of a dancer). Even while sitting watching TV there are some stretches you can do. Try the following (which are also great on a long-haul flight if you don't want to arrive at your destination as stiff as a board):

- Clench your buttocks and hold for ten seconds at a time and repeat as often as you like. No one will know you're doing it and it will give you buns of steel.

- Pull your knees up off the ground as high as you can while pointing your toes at the ground. Your thigh muscles (quadriceps) will tell you when to stop each repetition.

- Rotate each of your ankles five times clockwise and anticlockwise and repeat ad nauseam. You will strengthen their flexibility, which helps to guard against sprains.

- Stretch your arms up and out to the sides and across your chest. When stretching your right arm across your chest hold it in place with your left and vice versa.

- Keeping your back straight, lift up your legs and stretch them out before you until they are parallel with the ground (or as close as you can get to that). Your hamstrings will tell you when to stop each repetition so just hold the position for as long as you can.

- Draw your stomach in as far as you can and hold it for as long as you can. If it doesn't hurt after a while, you're not pulling it in enough. Repeat as often as you like.

HEALTHY QUOTES

THERE IS SOMETHING WRONG WITH A SOCIETY THAT DRIVES A CAR TO A WORKOUT IN THE GYM.

Bill Nye

• • • • • • • • •

WHEN I HEAR SOMEBODY SAY: 'LIFE IS HARD', I AM ALWAYS TEMPTED TO ASK: 'COMPARED TO WHAT?'

Sydney J. Harris

HEALTHY JOKES

WHATEVER YOU DO, ALWAYS GIVE 100 PER CENT. UNLESS YOU'RE DONATING BLOOD.

• • • • • • • • •

THE WORST TIME TO HAVE A HEART ATTACK IS WHEN YOU'RE PLAYING CHARADES.

• • • • • • • • •

A RECENT STUDY FOUND THAT WOMEN WHO CARRY A LITTLE EXTRA WEIGHT LIVE LONGER THAN THE MEN WHO MENTION IT.

• • • • • • • • •

THERE IS NOTHING WORSE THAN THAT AWKWARD MOMENT WHEN YOU'RE WEARING NIKES AND YOU JUST CAN'T DO IT.

GETTING PHYSICAL

If you want to exercise in more meaningful ways, you could think about taking up a sport or going back to one you used to enjoy before life got in the way, or going to the gym for some cardio or weight training, or getting back on your bike. Let's take a closer look at some of the many options open to us:

Cardio: the form of exercise that gets your heart pumping and your whole body moving, which is kind of what our bodies were designed to do in the first place, so it shouldn't really be too hard to do. It is, though, because we have evolved in the wrong direction altogether with our comfortable, often sedentary lifestyles. That's why cardio is also great for strengthening the muscles that move our bodies. Cardio sessions are available at everybody's local gym and of course you can do your own thing with basic activities like running or cycling.

Strength training: also widely referred to as 'pumping iron', strength training doesn't just build up your muscles like Popeye, it also improves your overall health and well-being. This is because it gets your metabolism and cardiac functions firing while strengthening your bones, tendons, ligaments and joints, as well as your all-important muscles.

HIIT: most gyms run HIIT (high-intensity interval training) sessions these days and there is a lot to be said for getting all your exercise in 30 minutes under the guidance of a personal trainer if you live a time-poor life. You can effectively do HIIT pretty much anywhere, though, because any burst of intense exercise from time to time during the day will reap benefits – just try running up two flights of stairs as quickly as you can and you'll get the idea.

Cycling: the activity that gives you all the exercise you want and makes you feel like a youngster again if you've been away from it for a while. It will give you aerobic benefit, added muscle and improved flexibility, but without the need to pound your poor legs on the road. You can also go quite far and see lots of interesting places while you're about it.

Swimming: whether you're into wild swimming, competitive swimming or just putting in some lengths for fun, there is nothing better than swimming to get worthwhile exercise without putting too much strain on your body. For that reason, it's also a really useful thing to do if you need to recover carefully from injury.

Running: some of the most goal-oriented people alive are runners, because they always want to improve on their previous best performances, whether over a short distance or over a marathon course (that's why they're always looking at their Fitbits to check their times, distances and calories burned). It is difficult to imagine anything more rewarding than finishing your first marathon, though, whatever your time was, and especially if you've done it in aid of a good cause. But beware, running is highly addictive. In a good way, though.

Triathlon: if you find running a marathon a bit too easy, try a triathlon, which will have you swimming over 1.5 km (0.93 miles) followed by a 40-km (25-mile) cycle followed by a 10-km (6-mile) run.

Ironman: if you find completing a triathlon a bit too easy, try an Ironman triathlon, which will enable you to stretch yourself out over a 3.9-km (2.4-mile) swim followed by a 181-km (112-mile) cycle followed by a full marathon-distance run of 42.2 km (26.2 miles). If you think this is still a bit too easy, you're an out-and-out liar.

Golf: because it is one of the most sociable games on earth, golf has a whole bunch of rules just to explain the etiquette that you should display towards your fellow players. But mostly it's just good old-fashioned exercise (especially if you walk the course), fresh air, elation (when you hit a good shot) and abject frustration (when you hit a bad one).

Team games: the great thing about being involved in team games is the camaraderie that goes with it, and of course the post-game beer. Whether rugby, basketball, hockey, (American) football, baseball, volleyball or cricket is your thing, they all have that camaraderie and beer to add to the enjoyment of actually playing the sport.

Martial arts: although some martial arts, like judo and karate, have evolved into competitive sports, they all have their origins in the ancient combat systems, strategies and philosophies of war. Today there are quite literally hundreds of them, although thankfully they are employed mostly to enhance fitness, health, confidence, moral values and spiritual well-being. Very few activities offer the human being that total package. Here are some of the more popular ones (with their original meanings in brackets) that you might like to look up online and try for yourself:

- Taekwondo (foot hand way)
- Judo (gentle, soft way)
- Karate (empty hand)
- T'ai chi ch'uan, aka t'ai chi (supreme ultimate boxing or exercise)
- Jiu-jitsu (soft, pliable method)
- Kung fu (time spent on hard training or endeavour)
- Kickboxing (a breakaway from karate)
- Muay Thai (Thai boxing, aka 'the art of eight limbs')

Yoga and Pilates: yoga seems to have taken over the world in recent times, so you might as well join in. The exercises will give you added strength, stamina, balance, flexibility and peace of mind. Pilates is great for developing your core strength because it focuses more on body alignment and posture.

HEALTHY EATING

I'm not going to waste time here telling you to watch your sugar and salt levels by moderating your intake of cakes, biscuits, pies and pastries, because you should know that already. Here are some reminders, though, about other tips that have been around for a while and which we all tend to forget on a regular basis:

Five a day: we all know the five-a-day rule, but we don't all know that it's about getting antioxidants into our system. To cut a long story short, oxidants don't like us. They try to do us harm, so we have to counteract them with the antioxidants found in fruit and vegetables and – here's the good news – red wine, coffee, tea and dark chocolate (but in moderation, of course). Best of all are colourful vegetables and fruit, which have more nutrients than paler ones.

Protein: keeps you going longer than carbs ever could, so don't be shy about frying up some bacon and eggs at any time of the day – just go easy on the toast – or about tearing into a chicken leg as a snack between meals, especially if you've earned that leg at the gym. Avocado, oily fish and skimmed milk are other good options (see also 'Superfoods').

Good carbs: not all carbs are as bad as bread and pasta, so do help yourself to a burst of manly energy with new potatoes, long-grain rice, sweet potatoes, apples and oranges, scrambled eggs on wholegrain bread and Greek yoghurt with blueberries (but not all on the same plate, obviously).

Find out what works for you: some people love nothing better than a hearty breakfast to get going in the morning; others can't face eating until lunchtime. Or you might prefer to eat little and often. Just eat what's good for you whenever it seems to best suit your metabolism and forget about the people who tell you that only one system can possibly work.

Shorten your eating window: finish eating and drinking (except for water) by 8 or 9 p.m. and go a good 12 hours overnight before having breakfast. This gives your body 12 whole hours to replenish itself and nibble away at your fat, especially if you drink lots of water during that time. If you don't fancy this as a lifestyle, try doing it once a week or just every now and then.

Portion control: we like to eat everything that's put in front of us, because good food shouldn't be allowed to go to waste. That's absolutely fine, as long as we don't pile the plate too high to begin with. There are lots of books and websites that will scientifically tell you how much of what you should eat, but common sense also works.

Superfoods: look out for so-called superfoods, which are becoming increasingly available as salads to eat in or take away, which means you don't even have to assemble the multiple ingredients yourself. Here are two common ones:

- Salads that contain some combination of couscous, quinoa, wheatgerm, legumes, nuts, seeds or beans, especially if mixed with some nice protein like avocado, salmon, chicken or egg.
- Fruit salads that contain blueberries, red berries, red or green grapes, kiwi fruit, pineapple or watermelon.

Superingredients: if you want to put 'superingredients' in your own cooking, use lots of olive oil, garlic, turmeric (curcumin) and ginger. 'Supervegetables' include sweet potatoes, mushrooms and seaweed. 'Superbreakfasts' could include banana, blueberries and high-fibre oats and cereals, all mixed together with Greek yoghurt.

Coffee: this is either bad for you or good for you, depending on who you care to listen to. It does a great job as an antioxidant and reduces the risk of contracting Alzheimer's or Parkinson's later in life, say some. It's a drug and it'll have you addicted in no time, say others. The truth is, most of us get by just fine on three or four cups a day with no ill effects. If you're worried about your caffeine levels, just drink the decaffeinated version every other time you have a coffee.

Recovery foods: great things to eat to help your body recover following vigorous exercise are salmon, tuna, chicken, eggs, watermelon and dark chocolate. And the even better news is that carbs also help the recovery process, so this is the time to treat yourself to some rice or pasta. No pain, no pasta!

VIVE LA DIFFERENCE!

In addition to the obvious differences, the male body is different in some other respects to that of the female species. Here's how:

A man's skin is 25 per cent thicker.

Men literally smell more. That's because we have more of the androsterone hormone, which is used by some animals to signal sexual and social information.

A man's face preserves its youthful appearance longer, because we lose collagen more slowly, making it more resistant to wrinkling and sagging. We generally throw away this natural advantage by not looking after our skin.

The male orgasm lasts an average of six seconds, compared with the average 23 seconds that women get. Unfair, but true.

No male body ever starts off as a male body, because the Y chromosome required to create one is inactive during the first five to six weeks of any embryo's life. It's our first opportunity to nurture our feminine side, except we always seem to sleep right through it.

Both men and women have cartilage structures to protect their vocal chords, but the male one starts to protrude more during the teenage years to allow for the voice to break and remain deeper thereafter. It is, of course, known as the Adam's apple.

Female bones complete their development around the age of 18, male bones around the age of 21. This explains why men generally have a higher forehead, larger jawbone and longer limbs.

Male pelvic bones are less round than female ones to avoid any suggestion that we should ever give birth to small humans (and we're far too busy doing manly things anyway).

The male body has evolved to recover from man flu in just a few months, whereas the female body takes days on end to recover from childbirth.

HEALTHY QUOTES

IF YOU WANT TO BE HAPPY, BE.

Leo Tolstoy

• • • • • • • • •

THERE IS MORE TO LIFE THAN INCREASING ITS SPEED.

Mahatma Gandhi

• • • • • • • • •

TIME YOU ENJOY WASTING IS NOT WASTED TIME.

Marthe Troly-Curtin

HEALTHY JOKES

MY THERAPIST SAYS I HAVE A PREOCCUPATION WITH VENGEANCE. WE'LL SEE ABOUT THAT.

· · · · · · · · ·

MY MOTHER MADE US TAKE ALL SORTS OF VITAMINS AND SUPPLEMENTS. ONE DAY I NEARLY CHOKED ON THE SUNDAY PAPERS.

· · · · · · · · ·

MY FRIEND GOT A PERSONAL TRAINER A YEAR BEFORE HIS WEDDING. I THOUGHT: 'BLOODY HELL. HOW LONG IS THE AISLE GOING TO BE?'

MENTAL HEALTH

Great strides are being taken these days to manage mental health in proactive and positive ways. This section looks at some of the obvious steps we can take to stay positive and finishes with a note on what to do if we need more help than a few tips.

Keep your brain active: positive mental activity even while young can help to stave off dementia later in life. Find enjoyable activities that stimulate you. Possibilities include crosswords, sudoku, learning new recipes, learning or brushing up on a foreign language and taking up a hobby. Pub quizzes are especially good, because they combine brain activity with social interaction and beer consumption.

Stay positive: do things that make you happy, and have regular 'me time' if there are things you like to do or places you like to go that are of limited interest to your partner. And smile. A lot.

Get a good night's sleep: if you need help getting to sleep, try a warm bath and maybe a short piece of yoga, Pilates, meditation or deep breathing before dropping off. More and more elite sportsmen are turning to yoga or Pilates as an essential addition to their regular training.

Power nap: you're either good at this or you're not. If you can doze off for 20–30 minutes and wake up fresh and raring to go, it will have done you the world of good in energising you for the rest of the day. If, on the other hand, you're the type that wakes up tired and grumpy, just forget it.

POWER HACK

A good trick to maximise your power nap is to have an espresso just before dozing off. The caffeine will be starting to kick in just as you come round in 20–30 minutes' time and you'll be firing on all cylinders for the rest of the day.

Get out of the house/office: you won't get much fresh air, sunlight or exercise sitting in front of the TV or your computer. If you haven't tried it for a while, you might be surprised at just how refreshing it can be to the mind, body and soul.

Be mindful: mindfulness is a wonderful thing. It involves taking the time to reminisce over the great times in your life, looking forward to the good times yet to come (e.g. your next holiday) and, most importantly, taking the time to be in the present. Look into meditation as a possible way to get you into the here and now. At the very least, you might learn to breathe more deeply, and you might be surprised to learn how important that is to your general well-being.

Breathe more deeply: I know what you're thinking, that human beings are really good at breathing because it's just what they do, but you couldn't be more wrong. In order to understand what deep breathing feels like, lie in bed and practise the 4–7–8 routine (breathe in for 4 seconds, hold your breath for 7 seconds and breathe out for 8 seconds). Here's what breathing more deeply does for you:

- *Increases energy:* oxygen doesn't just keep you alive; it replenishes your energy. The more oxygen, the more energy.
- *Improves your respiratory and cardiovascular systems:* breathing deeply relaxes the diaphragm, opens up the chest, improves your posture and minimises your risk of having a heart attack.
- *Relaxes your nerves and muscles:* relaxes you to the extent that your fight-or-flight responses are able to switch off, which in turn means less anxiety.
- *Offers protection from bacteria and viruses:* because the oxygen that circulates around your body is cleansing.
- *Improves your digestive system:* because the increased blood flow from the extra oxygen encourages your intestines to do their thing more efficiently.
- *Improves your mental state:* the brain needs a huge amount of oxygen to function properly. The more oxygen you give it, the more it will provide you with clarity of mind and purpose. It's a win-win situation.
- *Keeps you looking young:* it's true, breathing deeply increases the level of anti-ageing hormones released throughout your body.

Get a work–life balance that works for you: it's all very well being the guy who works hard and plays hard and hardly ever takes a holiday to prove how indispensable he is, but in Scandinavian countries such a person would be considered a moron. If you can't achieve what is expected of you during the length of a normal working week in these countries, it clearly means you are inefficient, bad at managing your own time and that of your team, and have no life of your own worth living. So, get a life. And keep it varied enough not to be that guy.

NOTE

The important thing to remember if life is getting you down for whatever reason is not to suffer in silence. Seek professional help at the earliest opportunity (it will always be confidential) and lean on your family and close friends, who would much rather help you in whatever ways they can than see you suffer or realise too late that there was something they could have done to help you through a difficult period. Just google 'mental health helplines' to find the sources you can reach out to if you think you need professional help.

ACKNOWLEDGEMENTS

My thanks to all the manly friends and family members who contributed their thoughts on how to be a real man in the twenty-first century, whether they were ultimately printable or not.

I am grateful to all at Summersdale Publishers, in particular to Robert Drew and Chris Turton on this occasion for their unwaveringly sound advice and editing. Thanks also to Emily Kearns for her thorough copy-editing and for being a pleasure to work with as always, and to Derek Donnelly for his meticulous final proofread.

DEDICATION

For Samuel Green, in celebration of him becoming an honest man.

ABOUT THE AUTHOR

A writer and editor of many years' standing, **Ray Hamilton** is able to draw on his wide experience of world travel, foreign languages and historical study to inform the subject matter of his work. His other books, all published by Summersdale, are as follows:

- *Military Quotations – Stirring Words of War and Peace* (2012)
- *Le Tour de France – The Greatest Race in Cycling History* (2013)
- *The Joy of Cycling* (2013)
- *The Joy of Golf* (2014)
- *Trains: A Miscellany* (2015)
- *M25: A Circular Tour of the London Orbital* (2015)
- *Knowledge: Stuff You Ought to Know* (2016)
- *A Short History of Britain in Infographics* (2017)
- *For the Love of the Navy* (2017)
- *For the Love of the Army* (2017)
- *Ride: A Fact-packed Tour through the World of Cycling* (2018)
- *For the Love of Trains: A Celebration of the World's Railways (2018)*

Cover & p.1 – bulb © Irina Adamovich/
Shutterstock.com; footballer © DVARG/
Shutterstock.com; suit © Panptys/
Shutterstock.com; knife and fork © i3alda/
Shutterstock.com; cogs © Summersdale
Publishers Ltd; aircraft © Rashad Ashurov/
Shutterstock.com; mouse © ScottMurph/
Shutterstock.com; heart © supanut
piyakanont/Shutterstock.com
Back cover – brain © Daria Sokolova/
Shutterstock.com; planet © FLUTES/
Shutterstock.com; atom © Summersdale
Publishers Ltd; mountain and sea ©
Merkushev Vasiliy/Shutterstock.com;
microscope © Alemon cz/Shutterstock.
com; helmet © Andrii_M/Shutterstock.
com; compass © Summersdale Publishers
Ltd; Palette and brush © Wiktoria Matynia/
Shutterstock.com
p.8 – © Alisa Ezediaro/Shutterstock.com
p.14 – © Vector SpMan/Shutterstock.com
pp.16–17 – © ZASIMOV YURII/
Shutterstock.com
p.19 – © pavlematic/Shutterstock.com
pp.24–25 – © bioraven/Shutterstock.com
p.29 – © SAK Design/Shutterstock.com
p.30 – © ArchMan/Shutterstock.com
p.44 – © Martial Red/Shutterstock.com
p.46 – © i3alda/Shutterstock.com
p.48 – © Summersdale Publishers Ltd
p.49 – © Summersdale Publishers Ltd
p.55 – © Reservoir Dots/Shutterstock.com
p.65 – © tuulijumala/Shutterstock.com
p.72 – © Digiart CT/Shutterstock.com
pp.82–83 – cutlery © Svetlana Drujinina/
Shutterstock.com; pasta © Sudowoodo/
Shutterstock.com
p.84 – © d1sk/Shutterstock.com
pp.87–97, 101, 102, 106 – knife and fork ©
i3alda/Shutterstock.com
p.99 – © Dmitriy Samorodinov/
Shutterstock.com
p.100 – © NEGOVURA/Shutterstock.com
p.104 – © Vectorcarrot/Shutterstock.com
p.105 – © Vectorcarrot/Shutterstock.com
p.110 – © ianlusung/Shutterstock.com
p.114 – © rikkyall/Shutterstock.com
pp.116–117, 122–123, 126–127, 130–131,
134–135 – cocktail icons © HappyPictures/
Shutterstock.com
p.120 – © larionova Olga 11/Shutterstock.com
p.130 – © Summersdale Publishers Ltd
p.132 – © pimlena/Shutterstock.com

p.136 – © Cube29/Shutterstock.com
p.138 – © Summersdale Publishers Ltd
p.145 – © Seita/Shutterstock.com
p.154 – © pixelliebe/Shutterstock.com
p.155 – © ednal/Shutterstock.com
p.156 – rugby ball © Martial Red/
Shutterstock.com; player © Nebojsa Kontic/
Shutterstock.com
p.157 – players © Nebojsa Kontic/
Shutterstock.com
pp.158–159 – bike chain © Tribalium/
Shutterstock.com
pp.158–159 – cyclists © KoQ Creative/
Shutterstock.com
p.160 – golf club © Tribalium/Shutterstock.
com; golf ball on tee © Rauf Aliyev/
Shutterstock.com
p.161 – golfer © Black creator/
Shutterstock.com
p.162 – cricket ball and wicket ©
Summersdale Publishers Ltd
p.163 – © Skocko/Shutterstock.com
p.164 – © Studio_G/ Shutterstock.com
p.166 – © Summersdale Publishers Ltd
p.169 – © ednal/Shutterstock.com
p.170 – © vectoric/Shutterstock.com
p.171 – © sabri deniz kizil/Shutterstock.com
p.182 – © Chipmunk131/ Shutterstock.com
p.183 – © Mr. Luck/ Shutterstock.com
p.184 – yellow design/Shutterstock.com
p.188 – © Yulia Yemelianova/
Shutterstock.com
p.189 – top left © InnervisionArt/
Shutterstock.com; top right © Sirtravelalot/
Shutterstock.com; bottom left © Ysbrand
Cosijn/Shutterstock.com; bottom right
© Antonio Guillem/Shutterstock.com
p.194 – © Baibaz/Shutterstock.com
p.195 – © Dmytro Boyko/Shutterstock.com
p.213 – KASUE/Shutterstock.com
p.214 – © Limbad/Shutterstock.com
p.215 – © Summersdale Publishers Ltd
pp.218–219 – © Nosyrevy/Shutterstock.com
p.222 – © Summersdale Publishers Ltd
p.232 – © Viktorija Reuta/Shutterstock.com
p.234 – © TroobaDoor/Shutterstock.com
p.240 – © kotss/Shutterstock.com
p.242 – © Panda Vector/Shutterstock.com
p.244 – © Roupplar/Shutterstock.com
p.245 – © 4ndrei/Shutterstock.com
pp.246–247 © TotemArt/Shutterstock.com
p.251 – © 90miles/Shutterstock.com
p.256 – © Panptys/Shutterstock.com

Have you enjoyed this book?

If so, why not write a review on your favourite website?

If you're interested in finding out more about our books, find us on Facebook at Summersdale Publishers and follow us on Twitter at @Summersdale.

Thanks very much for buying this Summersdale book.

www.summersdale.com